CIRCLES OF BLESSING

CIRCLES OF

BLESSING

William Carey Library
PASADENA • CALIFORNIA

By David A. Tucker
and Arlene Knickerbocker

Circles of Blessing:
Redemption in the Rain Forest

Unless otherwise noted, the Scripture quotations in this publication are from the King James Version of the Holy Bible. Scripture quotations noted NIV are from the Holy Bible: New International Version, 1973, 1978, 1984 by International Bible Society, Zondervan Publishing House, Grand Rapids, Michigan. Scripture quotations noted ANT are from the Holy Bible: The Amplified New Testament, 1958 by The Lockman Foundation, La Habra, California. Scripture quotations noted TLNT are from the Holy Bible: The Living New Testament, 1967 by Tyndale House Foundation, Wheaton, Illinois.

Published by
William Carey Library
PO Box 40129
Pasadena, California 91114
(626) 798-0819

William Carey Library
P.O. BOX 128-C • PASADENA, CALIFORNIA 91104

Library of Congress Cataloging-in-Publication Data

Tucker, David A., 1949-

Circles of blessing : redemption in the rainforest / by David A. Tucker and Arlene Knickerbocker.

p. cm.

ISBN 0-87808-605-6 (alk. paper)

1. Tucker, DavidA., 1949- 2. Tucker, Kathy, 1950- 3. Missionaries--Indonesia--Irian Jaya--Biography. 4. Baptists--Missions--Indonesia-Irian Jaya--History. 5. Missions--Indonesia--Irian Jaya--History--20th century. 6. Irian Jaya--(Indonesia)--Church History--20th century. I. Knickerbocker, Arlene, 1940- II. Title.

BV3342.T83 A3 2001
266'.0092'2--dc21
[B] 00-047779

Printed in the United States of America

Cover Design & Book Layout: D. M. Battermann — R&D Design Services

Contents

Foreword

For uncounted centuries two allied Irian Jaya tribes—the Kayagar and the Autohoim—survived within a menacing coil of enemies. With only brief respites, they fought Sawi to the north, Asmat to the west, Auyu to the east, or Yakai in the south. At last the Gospel of Christ, breaching walls of war, brought peace to both tribes and even, increasingly, to their enemies.

David and Kathy Tucker, bearers of that Gospel, experienced God's power enfolding the Kayagar, Autohoim and their own family of four within a community of heaven-sent blessing. What follows here is a remarkable first-person account of Christians doing what true Christians must seek to do, and do well—share God's Genesis 12:3 blessing with "all peoples on earth."

Don Richardson
Author of *Peace Child*; *Lords of the Earth*; and *Eternity in Their Hearts*

Preface

Circles of Blessing: Redemption in the Rain Forest is the wonderful story of God's redemptive work among the Kayagar people of Irian Jaya. Told by a gifted storyteller, it illustrates how God uses missionaries with all of our strengths and weaknesses to bring the gospel to the nations. It is the story of human weakness and divine power.

The book follows in the genre of *Peace Child*. It is autobiographical and told in the first person. It relates in dialogue and story form how God brings the light of the gospel to those who for centuries have lived in darkness. It is a thrilling account of a "people movement."

Circles of Blessing: Redemption in the Rain Forest is full of missiological insights, often gained by simply watching God at work! It shows how God used zealous, pioneering, impatient young missionaries to bring His message to the Kayagar people. We often learn more by our mistakes than in any other way! It traces the circles of blessings in the author's life and shows how God blessed him through others, and how he in turn reached a people who were totally unreached.

That is not the end of the story. The Kayagar people are now taking the gospel to their neighbors and even their former enemies. The Circles of Blessing continue. This is a good read and does not hide mistakes and failures while also showing the triumph of the gospel. God uses those who obediently venture forth to the ends of the earth to continue the Circles of Blessing.

Read, be challenged, and blessed!

Dr. Frank Severn,
General Director for SEND International

David Tucker is a good missionary and storyteller. In this brief autobiographical account of his ministry among the Kayagar and Autohoim in Irian Jaya, you will not only become involved with the stories, but with good missionary work.

As you read *Circles of Blessing: Redemption in the Rain Forest*, you will come to grips with faith and doubt, understanding and misunderstanding, good intuition and mistakes, victory and defeat, the human and the divine. You will feel like a front row observer in the remote village of Kawem. The book is written for the general audience, but Sunday school teachers and parents will also want to take the opportunity to read this story out loud to their children.

David appears in these pages exactly as I know him in our day-to-day working relationship. He came to work in the U.S. Office of SEND International in early 1994 as our Director of Recruitment. Currently he leads in the areas of training and short term ministries. He is a valued and vital member of our executive team. My prayer for you and many others is that this book be a blessing and encouragement to the church.

Dr. David B. Wood,
U.S. Director for SEND International

Acknowledgments

No author does his work alone. While my name is on the cover, many people contributed to this work through their encouragement, love, and practical helps. Most important to me was my co-author, Arlene Knickerbocker. Don Richardson was the first friend to suggest that I record this story. Arlene not only repeated that suggestion, but offered to help make it happen. Her initiative and perseverance made it possible for you to be reading this today.

My wife, Kathy, and daughters, Gwendolyn Heathcock and Kristen McLane, lived with me through the stories in this book. Kathy was as much a part of what God did as I was. Gwen and Kris witnessed God's power. Their memories and critical questions helped keep this story on course.

Having said thank you, I do want to make a dedication, or, more accurately, a series of dedications.

Charles Roberts, now walking in the presence of Christ, helped shape my life for God through his example and teaching. As Kathy and I graduated from Bible College, Charlie was the first person to join our support team and invest in our ministry.

Kipi was a simple Autohoim tribal woman in Irian Jaya, until now virtually unknown beyond her immediate family. In life, she was one of the first of her people to embrace Christianity. In death, her testimony brought many others into the kingdom.

Irina Novitsky is still alive and living in Ukraine. Her devotion to her Lord, her church and her country reminds me that God is at work throughout the world, in the cities as well as the jungles, continually calling out a people for His name.

To these friends past and present I lovingly dedicate this book.

Brief Biographical Sketches

DAVID A TUCKER, M.A.

David A. Tucker has been part of the missionary movement all of his adult life. He has an MA in Missions from Columbia Biblical Seminary. Dave and his wife, Kathy, served with Regions Beyond Missionary Union (RBMU) in Irian Jaya for nine years. During this time, the Tuckers saw six village churches established, a local Bible school program inaugurated, and national leaders appointed within the churches and Bible school. Currently, Dave is Director of Training and Short Term Ministries at SEND, International. He enjoys motivating Christians to reach out cross-culturally and training them to serve effectively.

ARLENE KNICKERBOCKER

Arlene Knickerbocker is a free-lance writer with an interest in missions. She writes for *Global Prayer Digest*. Arlene and her husband, Jerry, served as short term associates at Emmaus Road International in San Diego, an educational resource for cross-cultural ministry. Presently, Arlene is Director of Promotions at Manna Ministries, a local World Vision organization affiliated with LOVE, In the Name of Christ.

Introduction

BY ARLENE KNICKERBOCKER

God intends for blessings to flow in a circle. He can give us more blessings than we imagine, and He wants us to share these blessings with others. When we share them, this blesses God, Who blesses us again… Thus, we find ourselves in ***Circles of Blessing***.

God poured His love and blessings into Dave and Kathy Tucker until they were so saturated that love and blessing overflowed to others. Through the Tuckers, God moved two tribal groups from a cycle of fear into His circle of blessing.

While attending the "Perspectives on the World Christian Movement" course, I heard Dave share some of his experiences in Irian Jaya. When a woman asked, "Are your experiences in print?" Dave explained that he would like to have them in print but was too busy to get it done. "So if there is anyone here who would like to help me…?" I raised my hand. These stories blessed me and I am glad I can help pass on that blessing. Together we've produced ***Circles of Blessing: Redemption in the Rain Forest***, which we hope provides you with:

Information on:
- God's sufficiency.
- Global outreach.
- Cultural diversity.

Encouragement by seeing how-
- God blessed Dave and Kathy.
- God blessed people in Irian Jaya.
- God can bless you.

Motivation to-
- Praise God.
- Pray for others.

Peer into your heart and see God working.

With the angels we repeat, "Worthy is the Lamb that was slain to receive power, and riches, and wisdom, and strength, and honor, and glory, and blessing" Revelation 5:12.

IRIAN JAYA

IRIAN JAYA

"But ye shall receive power, after the Holy Spirit is come upon you; and ye shall be witnesses unto me both in Jerusalem, and in all Judea, and in Samaria, and unto the uttermost part of the earth" Acts 1:8.

As technology seized most of the world, many hidden people still lived in a stone-age culture. Tribal people, driven by fear, fought fiercely and cannibalized their victims.

Early in the 20th century, explorers penetrated Dutch New Guinea. This area became known as West Irian. For many years, we knew this country as Irian Jaya (literally, Glorious Irian), part of the Indonesian government. In 2000, Irian Jaya became West Papua (aka Indonesian New Guinea). Papua New Guinea and West Papua together make up the second largest island in the world. In this book, the country is called Irian Jaya.

By 1975, when Dave and Kathy Tucker moved to Irian Jaya, the tribal people accepted outsiders because of material goods. Yet God provided blessings far beyond what they expected.

Pacific Ocean
Kalimantan (Borneo)
Sumatra
West Papua (Irian Jaya)
Java
Indian Ocean
Arafura Sea

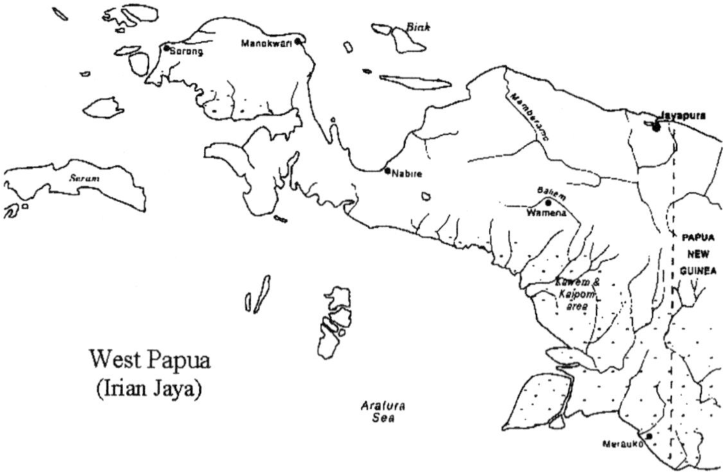
Sorong
Manokwari
Biak
Mamberamo
Jayapura
Seram
Nabire
Baliem
Wamena
PAPUA NEW GUINEA
Kawem & Kaipom area
West Papua
(Irian Jaya)
Arafura Sea
Merauke

CHAPTER ONE

God Gives Peace

"Dave," my wife, Kathy, called, "I'm dressing Gwen; can you get Kristen out of bed?"

As I pulled back the mosquito netting and lifted my youngest daughter out of her crib, I heard a cough outside the screened window. Usually that meant someone wanted my attention.

I looked out the window to see my first caller of the day. Next to a sago palm tree stood Andreas, a man from the nearby village of Kawem. Andreas was tall and lithe with glistening, black hair. His smile ended at a curved bone protruding from his pierced nose. I waved and almost turned away—then I did a double take.

Sweat ran freely down his painted face and naked body. Looking more closely, I noticed he was cradling his left arm and showing me a jagged, round wound, which was oozing blood. It looked as if he had been shot with an arrow.

Oh, no, I thought, *he wants me to sew up his arm. I've done some minor medical work, but this will be a challenge.*

I began thinking about the bigger picture. *Where is the other guy? Maybe the fight didn't involve just two people. How many others are there?* Then it hit me. *He's smiling like that because he's proud of getting wounded in battle.*

"Oh Lord," I prayed in silent desperation. "Please help!" Then I called, "Kathy, can you watch Kristen now? There's an emergency, and I need to go to the clinic."

I rushed outside and led Andreas to the porch of my clinic,

cleaned the wound, and sewed it up the best I could with my limited medical training.

We had come to Kawem village because of the people's spiritual needs, but we couldn't ignore their physical suffering. So I had learned some basic medical treatment from another cross-cultural worker and opened a "clinic" about one hundred yards from our house.

My clinic was a six-by-eight foot bark-covered building held three feet off the ground by stilts because of frequent flooding. Shelves full of supplies covered one wall. During clinic time each day, I removed a two-by-three foot window in the front wall so people could stand near the window on the narrow porch and tell me what was wrong—mostly coughs, colds, aches, bacterial infections, or skin diseases common to the tropical rain forest. I dispensed cough syrup, aspirin, antibiotics, and anti-fungal cream as needed. I also handed out vitamins as a general policy, since the people's diet in this area lacked proper nutrients.

Friends carried the seriously ill to an area sheltered by an awning, where I examined and treated them. Sometimes people came to my home because of an emergency. Occasionally people led me to a bedridden family member.

Even in this crude setting with few medical credentials, I provided better health care than people from the Kayagar tribe were getting using their traditional methods. Without my help, they had no access to any of these medicines. They had never heard of bacterial or viral infections. They didn't know it was important to keep wounds clean. As I helped physically, and even saved some lives, I was building relationships which allowed me to share the gospel message.

Today I faced new challenges. I worked on Andreas, knowing he would not be my only patient. Kayagar families closed ranks when one of their members got into a fight. Whether those fighting were right or wrong, families stood loyally behind them. These clans didn't like to stop fighting until the score was even; and that meant at least two wounded (or killed), usually many more. Sure enough, other wounded people from Kawem trailed to my clinic looking for treatment.

Kayagar was the name these people used to include all who spoke *Boup Nohom* (our tongue). Several villages, each made up of two or three extended families or clans, comprised the Kayagar tribe. The Kayagar seldom war within their own clans, so I thought another village besides Kawem was probably involved. I soon learned from my patients that it was.

Amaru, about a mile up the Cook River, was the other village. I had already seen many wounded Kawem warriors. I knew large numbers of wounded suffered in Amaru too, and they were a day's canoe trip from medical treatment unless they could get past the Kawem guards between Amaru and my clinic. I pictured injured men stumbling along the path reaching out their bloody arms for help. I knew they couldn't get to me, and I couldn't get to them either.

The fighting has to stop, I thought throughout the morning, *but who can stop it?*

The answer to my question had poked at my consciousness, but focusing on immediate medical needs kept it from surfacing. When I got a break, the question rose again; and abruptly, the answer came to me—*I was the logical choice!* The Indonesian government only became involved with remote villages as a last resort. By then, most of the people might be dead. *But, what should I do? What could I do?*

I walked toward Kawem village. The huts made from sago palm fronds still slouched in two rows divided by the silty path; but where was the grayish-blue smoke that usually drifted lazily from each hut, leaving its smell on everything it touched? Where were the women and children? Were they hiding in the forest?

The air nearly crackled with tension. All able-bodied men clustered at the far end of the village. Some of them were barely fourteen years old. They looked different decorated for war. I had only seen this type of dress during a couple of village dances. With a sickening feeling, I realized those entertaining dances had actually been reenactments of past battles. A chill ran through my body despite the hot midday sun.

I noticed the bones and pig tusks sticking through their pierced noses and ears. Some wore necklaces made from animal teeth. Red and white paint decorated their faces and bare chests with clan symbols, an appeal to clan spirits for strength and protection. I had heard the steady monotone of drums beating all morning; now I noticed how this war beat provided an emotional background for the agitated hum coming from the warriors. Another storm of violence was brewing, and the only hope for calming it was to act quickly.

At that moment I cursed my vivid imagination. The stories I had heard about Kayagar warfare became very real to me; visions of brutal murder and cannibalism flashed through my mind. *That is what they might do to each other!* I thought.

How will they receive me? Will they be angry if I interfere? I would soon find out, but first I had to talk with Kathy. I turned toward our house.

Throughout the morning, Kathy and the girls had stayed inside. We didn't seem to be in direct danger, but flying arrows and spears don't always land on target. I'd gone to our house as often as I could to tell Kathy the latest news. This time I had to tell her I planned to intercede.

Kathy met me at the door with a hug. "Dave, I've been on the missionary radio network asking our RBMU coworkers to pray. Should I ask for a missionary plane to evacuate us? I really don't think we should run away, but I'm not sure what else we can do."

"I'm not sure what to do either." My reply wasn't much help. "But we can't leave now. It might be good to get you and the girls out later today if things don't quiet down. Right now, we're needed here. I'm not a great medic, but I'm better than nobody. More than that, I think I have to try to stop this fighting. There have been several small skirmishes already, and now they're getting ready for a big battle. I don't feel very brave right now, but this is part of the reason we're here in Kawem. I'm going to talk to the men."

"What will you say?"

I wished I had an answer for Kathy's practical question; but I could only reply, "I don't know what to say, and my Kayagar language skills aren't great either. I hope God leads me to say the right things and helps them understand me."

"What set this off?"

"From what I can piece together," I responded, "some teenagers from Kawem and Amaru were playing soccer in a field about halfway between the villages. The play got rough, and somebody was knocked down and hurt."

"That doesn't sound like a good reason to start a war," Kathy said as she picked Gwen up and held her close.

"That was only the beginning. The brother of the boy who was hurt hit the one who did the pushing. Then his family remembered a fight about five years ago. Families and friends began taking sides. Yelling and pushing gave way to fist fights. Others heard the skirmish and ran to the site. Soon arrows flew—and well, you've seen the results as people came to the clinic this morning."

"It seems so ridiculous to fight like this over a soccer game," Kathy said, "and then to bring up an old argument and start shooting each other with arrows. Now it looks as though it might turn into a full tribal war."

"I agree, Kak, but I'm learning that these people have long memories. They find their identities in what they can remember about their past. This is a horrible way to learn about the Kayagar culture, but seeing this fight is helping me understand the way they think."

"So you think you have to get involved right now?" Kathy's wistful glance told me she was as uneasy as I was.

"Yes. Please pray for me as I talk to them. I am scared! I know I can't do this on my own. We desperately need God's help."

I crossed the short footbridge from our yard into Kawem. As if on cue, the head of every warrior swiveled in my direction. As I began my trek toward them, my emotional state made it seem even hotter than the one-hundred degree weather I had come to expect.

What am I doing here? The thought popped into my head suddenly.

Sometimes the mind does funny things and dredges up seemingly unrelated thoughts and events. In the middle of a village path, halfway around the world from where I considered home, I remembered asking myself the same question during my first year of college. *What am I doing here?* Feeling confused and aimless, I had searched for an answer. Since I could find no good answer, I had left the school.

Should I quit now? Should I just go back to the United States, find a good job, and live comfortably? Why should I keep patching up injuries these people are bringing upon themselves? Why should I subject my family to this heat, inconvenience, and danger? Why am I here instead of in a clean, safe, air-conditioned office?

No, I'm not going to quit. This time I have an answer to why I am here. God sent me. He gave me love for these people and hatred for the deceiver who causes them pain. God gave me purpose and led me to this spiritual battlefield for a reason. God gave me plans to convey eternal hope through the gospel of Christ. God gave me peace. I feel confident God is present and in control. I've read the Book; I know I'm on the winning side in this spiritual warfare.

My contemplation confirmed my commitment. It also made the walk through the village pass quickly. All too soon I stood before the men of Kawem.

First I noticed the weapons in their hands: seven-foot wooden spears tipped with the sharp toenails of large cassowary birds, four-foot bamboo arrows tipped with a six-inch barbed wooden point, and long steel knives called *parangs*.

The men greeted me with silence. I looked around the circle of warriors. Some eyes opened wide with fear and others blazed with rage. Some hands trembled noticeably while others gripped their weapons so hard their knuckles were nearly white. Jaws clenched. Veins stood out. Nostrils flared.

My heart beat frantically. I took a deep breath, swallowed the lump in my throat, and prayed a silent "Help!"

God's peace that passes understanding flowed over me, and I spoke without a tremble in my voice. "*Yahanap-yahanap* (friends), are you going to battle with Amaru?"

"Yes," several replied in unison. All heads nodded emphatically.

"You know many of you will be injured or die."

"Yes, we know."

Obviously, they wouldn't respond to fear.

Next I pleaded, "Please don't do this. It will only bring harm and no good."

One of the older men leaned against his spear and stolidly said, "We must avenge the injuries suffered so far."

How could I persuade them to stop fighting? I was jumping from subject to subject, speaking in terse sentences with lots of accompanying hand motions. So far, they seemed to understand what I was saying.

"I don't want to have my family living in such a dangerous place where they could be hurt during your battle. If I leave, who will help you when you're sick and injured?"

As I racked my brain for other negative consequences, I remembered some recent events in the highlands of Irian Jaya when the army came in with a heavy hand and burned many villages to the ground.

"Willem." I singled out a government teacher who had recently traveled through that area and seen the devastation firsthand. "Remember when you saw every hut burned in the villages that were rebellious? Do you want the Indonesian army to do that in Kawem?"

Everyone turned to Willem. He looked at his feet, then at me.

"Yes, I saw that."

His eyes scanned the village stopping briefly at his family's home. "That would not be a good thing to happen here."

They began talking among themselves. Though I couldn't understand all their words, I could tell that their tone was less harsh. I think many of them wanted an honorable way to step out of the cycle of revenge and battle.

After a moment, I finished with some bargaining. Usually, the people gave me food or some type of small payment for treating them. "Some of your wounded men have already come to me for treatment, but the men from Amaru are afraid to travel here. It's not fair for me to treat your wounds but not theirs. If you will stop fighting now, I will give free medical treatment to people from both Kawem and Amaru."

After another discussion, the men nodded and agreed to stop fighting.

I wiped the sweat from my brow and breathed a prayer of thanks.

I knew without God's continued intervention, this peace was temporary, since their belief system promoted war. The Kayagar people believed when they died, their spirit only stayed alive as long as others remembered them. Outlandish actions helped people tell stories and remember. Since deceit was a virtue in their eyes, people tried to outdo one another with treachery. Kayagar warriors fought with the hope of becoming heroes, even legends.

The Kayagar's credence also promoted fear. They could never trust one another. To build their reputation, people always tried to deceive and harm others. Once they deceived or harmed someone, that person's family and friends felt obligated to avenge the deed. And so the cycle continued.

Fear of spirits hovered like a dark cloud over the Kayagar. They never knew when that cloud would burst and rain down misery on them. If they forgot someone who had died, the person's spirit could cause enough trouble for them to remember. Whenever anything bad happened, the Kayagar people thought a spirit caused it and recalled those who had died.

Since it was hard to remember departed ones without pictures or written documents, human bones served as functional reminders. In the world from which I came, children playing with their grandfather's skull would be unthinkable and gruesome. Here skulls often served as toys or pillows; small bones and teeth made wall decorations or jewelry; larger, stronger bones were shaped and filed into lethal weapons. People used these bones as reminders of their dead loved ones in hopes of placating the spirits.

Even though I had heard about children playing with shiny skulls before I came to Irian Jaya, it still affected me greatly each time I saw it. Seeing a little boy with fingers inserted in the eye sockets and rolling a skull like a bowling ball quickly reminded me the Kayagar way of looking at everything was completely alien to me. *Since they saw everything from such a different perspective, would I ever communicate God's Word to them effectively?*

My heart hurt when I thought of the cycle of war and fear that enslaved the Kayagar and other people. *If only they could realize we can live in peace with God forever. If only they knew God was trustworthy. If only...*

Soon there was no more time to ponder. I sent a messenger to the Amaru people with my "free treatment" offer. Though I had prepared the clinic, I was not ready emotionally for the onslaught of work that followed. Canoes full of injured came. Often I just cleaned and bandaged a wound, but I closed some of them with a sterile sewing needle and white thread. Arm after arm received a shot of penicillin to combat possible infection. I gave aspirin to those in great pain and vitamins to all.

Wayrem, a man from Amaru, had an arrow wound deep in his chest. Kayagar arrowheads had barbs carved into them. These arrowheads did more damage coming out than going in. As was their custom, someone had crudely removed this arrow by inserting a piece of wood next to it and loosening each barb. That expanded the wound and increased risk of infection.

Maybe I should have sent Wayrem by missionary plane to a real hospital, but I saw his need and began working on him immediately. I did everything I could think of and then consulted by radio with a missionary doctor. I cleaned the wound, left it draining, and pumped him full of antibiotics. I instructed his family about continued care and visited him regularly to change dressings and give more antibiotics.

Wayrem hung in the balance for about two weeks. Kathy and I prayed fervently for his life. If he died, the fighting might start the cycle of revenge going again. Finally, it became obvious that Wayrem would live. Day by day his strength increased, and one day Wayrem asked his friends to help him get down river to visit me.

Kathy and I saw Wayrem standing on our porch, weakly gripping the railing. "Tuan Dafid," he called faintly, "I have to talk to you."

Kathy ran to the door and helped him inside. He staggered to our kitchen table and collapsed into a chair.

"*Terima Kasih*," he breathed.

I almost fell off my chair. No Kayagar had ever before thanked me. In fact, the Kayagar language didn't even have a word for thank you. They had adopted these Indonesian words to express thanks.

"Dafid, I know I would have died without your help," he continued in the Kayagar language.

I opened my mouth, but he stopped me before I could say anything.

"Wait. I have to say this. While I lay on the mat in my house, I did not know if I would live or die. If I died, I did not know where I would be. Yes, Dafid, I know our stories about death, but I was still afraid. I don't ever want to feel that scared again. Tell me about your God."

Kathy and I listened in stunned silence. While we had been so busy concentrating on physical healing, God had used this situation to bring spiritual healing, too. It was satisfying to play a part in Wayrem's physical healing, but God gave us an even greater blessing when He let us lead this seeker to Him, the great Physician Who heals spiritual wounds.

That day God lifted the heavy burden of sin off Wayrem, dissolved the cloud of fear that had hung over him, and filled his heart with peace. Wayrem learned that he didn't have to work hard and do great deeds to live forever, he could just accept God's love and forgiveness by faith in what Christ had done. Wayrem placed his trust in someone for the first time, and that Someone would never fail him.

"Wayrem, I have even more wonderful news for you," I told him after his prayer. "Your name is written in God's Book of Life, and He will remember you always. You will live in heaven forever."

He asked some questions and I read from Luke, telling him how God gives His children power over evil spirits. "Notwithstanding, in this rejoice not, that the spirits are subject unto you; but rather rejoice, because your names are written in heaven" Luke 10:20.

I read from Revelation 20:12, "And I saw the dead, small and great, stand before God, and the books were opened; and another book was opened, which is the book of life..." Then verse 15, "And whosoever was not found written in the book of life was cast into the lake of fire."

We continued reading chapter 21, rejoicing that God said He would dwell with His people forever and take away all death, sorrow, and pain.

From that day, Wayrem's heart overflowed with thanksgiving; and he began serving God from gratitude rather than serving spirits from fear. He had moved from the cycle of battle into God's circle of blessing.

CHAPTER ONE APPLICATION GUIDE

"Be anxious for nothing, but in everything, by prayer and supplication with thanksgiving, let your requests be made known unto God. And the peace of God, which passeth all understanding, shall keep your hearts and minds through Christ Jesus" Philippians 4:6-7.

It's easy, when thrown into an alien environment, to worry and feel stressed out. "Be anxious for nothing" is a command we can follow only through exercising faith. Though Dave found himself surrounded by hostile warriors carrying spears, he persevered because of his confidence in God. That doesn't mean Dave had no fear; but he was able to see beyond the angry faces, war paint, and sharpened spears. He fixed his eyes on his loving, powerful Father.

You and I probably won't ever face that type of situation, but we face stress every day. Can we have peace in our hearts when illness strikes, when money runs out, when those we love hurt us? Through faith in God, we can.

Focusing on God's character makes us realize He is worthy of our trust in good times and in bad. Reading the Bible and learning how God helped ordinary people overcome fear and do great things strengthens our faith. Exercising our faith brings opportunities to experience God's great power.

The more we get to know God, the more we trust Him. The more we trust God, the more we get to know Him. What a wonderful circle of blessing.

"When a train goes through a tunnel and it gets dark, you don't throw away your ticket and jump off. You sit still and trust the engineer." *Corrie ten Boom.*

PONDER these Scriptures:

Psalm 29:11; Ephesians 2:14-18; James 3:18.

PRAISE God for peace.

Read John 14:27 and consider the kind of peace God gives.

Read Isaiah 26:3 and thank God for inner contentment when we praise Him.

PEER into your heart.

Are you confident God is in control? Do you believe he

will never abandon you?

What worries hide in your heart? Are you relying on your own strength for help?

Focus on God's power and hand over these worries to Him.

PRAYER

Peaceful Father, I praise You for Your peace which doesn't depend on circumstances. Through this day help me place my hand in Yours and look to You in trust. Thank You that there is nothing I have to face in my own strength. I pray for those whose minds and lives are full of turmoil. May they learn about Jesus Christ, the Prince of Peace. Help missionaries around the world take courage from Your presence as they share the gospel of peace with those who don't know You. Help me faithfully proclaim Your peace to those around me. Amen.

CHAPTER TWO

God Gives Love

I stood on the welcome mat of the big, yellow house and rang the doorbell. My hopes lifted when the door opened. There stood a pleasant-looking lady wearing a soft, blue blouse that matched her eyes.

"Hi! I'm David. A new kingdom is coming soon. Do you know about this? May I show you an article in this magaz…"

"Are you a Jehovah's Witness?" she interrupted.

"Yes, but…"

The door slammed shut before I could finish. I stepped off the welcome mat.

My partner, a tall African-American man, patted my slumped shoulder and said, "You tried, David. Let me tell you what to say at the next house."

I shuffled away asking myself, *What am I doing here?* I didn't realize the same question would repeat itself throughout my life. This time I didn't have a good answer; it was just something my family did.

Every Saturday and Sunday morning, rain or shine, we met others at the Kingdom Hall. Our group leader, my father, dispersed us in pairs and assigned a target area of town. We spent the next couple of hours going door-to-door trying to distribute copies of our magazines. I decided there was one good thing about going–Dad gave me two cents for each magazine I sold. If I sold enough *Watchtowers* and *Awakes*, I could buy some candy and maybe even go to a movie. As a ten-year-old, I had simple goals.

Even as a youngster, questions rose about Jehovah's Witness doctrines and teaching. When I didn't get satisfactory answers to my questions, they turned to nagging doubts.

"Mom," I asked more casually than I felt, "Grampie and Grammie drink the wine and eat the bread at Kingdom Hall every year, but no one else in our family does that. Why?"

"They are part of the 144,000 witnesses the Bible talks about in the book of Revelation."

"But how do they know they are part of the 144,000?"

She glanced up from the clothes she was folding and said softly, "They just know."

That answer didn't satisfy me.

Later I read Revelation 7:4-8 and realized the 144,000 witnesses will be from the twelve tribes of Israel. My grandparents on my father's side didn't qualify.

The strict rules we followed as Jehovah's Witnesses often separated me from my friends. All through my childhood I didn't understand why I couldn't celebrate Christmas or my birthday. Each school day while all the other kids recited the Pledge of Allegiance to the American flag, I stood in respect but stayed silent.

"David, why aren't you repeating the Pledge of Allegiance?" various teachers asked.

"I'm a Jehovah's Witness, and we don't pledge allegiance to any nation." I knew the words but wasn't sure what they really meant.

Besides the Saturday and Sunday morning works, we sat through one-hour lectures at the Kingdom Hall four or five times a week. At least there I felt a part of the group. As I sat surrounded by grandparents, parents, brothers, sisters, aunts, uncles, and cousins, I felt comfortable and accepted—as long as I followed the rules. I heard adults talking about others who had not followed the rules, and how leaders excommunicated them from our fellowship. That seemed the worst possible punishment.

My grandfather spoke at the Kingdom Hall regularly. I remember one sermon in particular because it scared me. It ended, "...and so we'll leave the plane that was lost in the storm. We must not be like this pilot who wasn't prepared for death. We must be doing good works continually, because we never know when the end will come."

My father nodded in agreement; he often spoke at the Kingdom Hall, too. Following in their footsteps, I looked for opportunities to read aloud from the Bible, answer questions, and speak up whenever I could. All ages met together, but if the main auditorium got too crowded, sometimes a smaller group moved into a side room. I always volunteered to go with the smaller group because it offered more opportunities for me to show what I had memorized.

"Why did King Nebudchadnezzer lose his throne?" My father looked up from the podium.

My hand shot up as high as I could reach.

"David, do you have an answer?" Dad tried not to call on me too often. He knew I had the answer because he had helped me underline the answers in the magazine just that afternoon.

Even after reading the answers, questions still plagued me like a toothache. This might have become a crisis as I grew older, but that crisis never developed.

As my father began working longer hours in a new job, we stayed home from Kingdom Hall meetings more and more. The new job brought many changes—even a move.

My youngest brother, Tim, pressed his nose against the car window and waved at the only home we remembered. He whispered, "Goodbye house." I put my arm around his small shoulders. He was two and I was twelve. We were leaving for our new house in Park Ridge, New Jersey. I was sad, too; but I had to keep my sadness inside because I was the big brother.

After this move, our family life altered drastically. We never again attended a meeting at the Kingdom Hall. We didn't talk about it; we just didn't go. We had more free time, and we started looking and acting like our friends.

Timidly I joined my classmates for the first time. "I pledge allegiance... Oh, say, can you see by the dawn's early light..."

Then at Christmas, we wondered what would happen. "Merry Christmas," my mother said tentatively. We followed her lead and enjoyed this new experience, though it was only a secular holiday to our family then. We celebrated simply with no tree or decorations. My sisters saw me looking at a catalog and whispered, "Do you think we'll get presents?"

I answered, "I'm letting Mom and Dad know I want a shooting gallery just in case. A few days before Christmas I heard popping noises coming from my dad's study, and that special morning I had my turn to play with the first present I ever received—the shooting gallery.

As was common in our family, we went to extremes the following Christmases. Our house glowed with colored lights inside and out; and we gave up a quarter of our living room to tree, decorations, and wrapped presents.

Other changes came that were less satisfying. The Bible had been a major reference in our lives, but now our Bibles lay unused. I no longer had any authority, other than my parents, on which to base my choices.

I was sixteen when I felt drawn to read the Bible on my own, looking for answers to normal teenage struggles. I got as far as the fifth chapter of Genesis, but my curiosity didn't get me through the first list of *begats*. I put the book back on the shelf. Too bad, because I would soon need its wisdom even more.

"Davy," my father's words penetrated my Saturday morning sleepiness.

"Davy?" He hadn't called me that for years.

"I know I was going to take you to play basketball today, but we can't go."

I had almost expected this. I had been surprised when he enrolled us in a father-son basketball league. I was happy but afraid to believe him—to face more disappointment in our relationship. Dad had been spending more and more time away from home. When he was home, he was silent unless he and Mom were arguing.

"Davy, you know your mother and I have problems; but no matter what happens, I love you. I'm leaving now, but I will come back. You can count on me."

We hugged. We cried. This was the first time I remember seeing my dad shed a tear. Even though I doubted his return, I wanted to believe him. I thought, *This morning proves how much I can count on you. You drop this on me and then run away*. But I said, "We have each other."

He did come back, but the day came when he moved out permanently; and eventually my parents divorced.

Money was tight then, and my mom began looking for a job.

As a high school dropout without recent job experience, she didn't have many options. She cleaned homes and took in laundry until she landed a job as a sales clerk in a local department store.

Mom continued to read the classified ads, and one day she saw an ad that would change our lives forever. The First Baptist Church of Pascack Valley needed someone to manage their nursery. Mom liked children and Sunday morning was free. They would even provide transportation. We didn't think they would hire a Jewish woman who converted to the Jehovah's Witness persuasion when she married. But they did. Though we didn't know it then, the pastor looked for such God-given opportunities to draw people into God's family.

"Ding, Dong." This time I wasn't ringing the doorbell, I was answering it.

I recognized Bruce Allen, the young red-haired pastor. In the few months since Mom had begun working in the nursery, I had met Pastor Allen several times. My sisters and one brother had often gone with Mom on Sunday morning, first helping in the nursery then sitting in the church services. I preferred to sleep on Sunday morning.

"Hi, Dave. I'm here to pick up Taffy and Roberta." Noticing my glance toward his car full of teenagers, he offered, "Hey, why don't you come with us; we're going to a movie in Paterson." When I hesitated, he added, "It's free."

"Why not? I'll grab my jacket and be right there," I answered.

"Let's sit in the balcony," someone suggested as we walked into the semi-darkened theater.

We watched "The Restless Ones" produced by the Billy Graham organization. It was the first Christian film I'd ever seen. The story was inspiring, and I enjoyed watching it; but I looked at it purely as entertainment.

"It's over. Let's hurry and beat the rush," I whispered loudly.

"Stay here, Dave," Pastor Allen said. "We're not finished yet."

The lights came up, and a man stepped onto the stage. "Now Billy Graham will speak to us."

I recognized the name of this famous "religious guy." The film had featured him helping the characters resolve some problems in their lives. I was curious enough to sit forward at this announcement.

The man continued, "Dr. Graham isn't here with us personally, but he will talk to us through a recording."

A tape recording. I almost exclaimed out loud, *How crummy.*

I wasn't expecting the life-changing message I heard next. For the first time I heard a clear gospel message and God's Holy Spirit went to work on me.

"You are a sinner," came the words from the tape.

Yeah, I would agree with that.

"Christ died to pay the penalty for your sin."

Wow! I didn't understand how that worked, but the thought impressed me powerfully.

"You can receive eternal life and peace with God by accepting Christ as your personal Savior. Every head down, every eye closed," Billy Graham continued. "If you accept His offer of salvation, pray with me now."

I drank in every word and didn't hesitate to respond. This is what I had been seeking.

"If you have prayed this prayer tonight, please stand where you are."

How could I lose? I stood.

When I opened my eyes, I was surprised that people were still in their seats. *Why would anyone refuse such an offer?* I thought. Now I realize many in the crowd had already accepted Christ, but it still amazes me that people refuse such an offer.

The tape ended and the man on the platform said, "If you have prayed this prayer with Dr. Graham, I want you to come forward and stand with me."

As I made my way toward the platform that evening, I saw Taffy and Roberta also hurrying down the aisle.

"Hello, my name is Mr. Carroll. Tell me what happened to you tonight."

"I think I have eternal life," I told him.

A mature Christian, Mr. Carroll was there to counsel people who were placing their trust in Christ. He helped reinforce my new belief and commitment. "That's great! Let me show you this verse in God's Word. 'For God so loved the world, that He gave His only begotten Son, that whosoever believeth in Him should not perish, but have everlasting life' John 3:16. Have you believed in Jesus, Dave?"

"Yes, that's what I just did."

"Then what has God done for you?"

"I think He gave me eternal life."

"Do you just think that, Dave, or are you sure?"

"If God wrote that in His Word, then it must be true. I am sure." I was speaking as much to myself as to Mr. Carroll.

He led me through some other verses. Then he prayed with me and gave me my own copy of John's Gospel and some other literature.

God did a recreative work in me that night. Genesis chapter one says the earth was without form and void in the beginning. That described how I felt about my life before that night. It, too, was without shape and purpose. Darkness covered spiritual truths. When the Holy Spirit of God moved over me, God opened my spiritual eyes; and I saw (understood) spiritual truths for the first time. God breathed His life into me and my dead spirit came to life.

Taffy and Roberta also experienced new life that night. My brother, Brett, soon accepted Jesus, and we four were baptized that New Year's Eve, 1966. When "The Restless Ones" was shown a year later, I counseled someone else who responded. This was my first opportunity to draw another into God's circle of blessing.

I didn't comprehend all that happened to me when I became God's child, but I did realize my Heavenly Father loved me. Soon I noticed the love He poured into me spilling over to others.

Years later in the highlands of Irian Jaya, I saw an abundance of pure water flowing out of a mountainside. This spring became a favorite place for our family to visit. Many others also stopped to drink in the beauty and wonder where all this cool water originated. It was a beautiful and welcome sight in a hot land where polluted water was the norm.

When I saw this spring, I couldn't help thinking that God's love can flood our lives and flow over onto all who come around us, too. Unconditional love is refreshing in a "me first" society. It is unusual—supernatural—everyone who sees it wonders where this love originates. Loving gives us opportunities to tell people about God. Loving identifies us as Christians. "By this shall all men know that ye are my disciples, if ye have love one to another" John 13:35.

I didn't realize all that then; but I did know Someone loved me unconditionally. If I was grumpy or had a pimple or didn't obey every rule perfectly, it didn't affect God's love. I responded with joy.

In His unconditional love, I found a significance and security I'd never known before. I knew my family loved me, but they couldn't help displaying some of the conditional love they had learned through the years.

As far as girls went, I'd been "in love" before. I found a new object for my affection every week. I was a romantic and liked any girl who looked at me twice (sometimes even once).

My infatuations usually didn't last long, however, because the girl usually didn't feel the same. Now that I understood love better, I began to look at girls differently. Before that, I had listened to the other boys tell about which girls made them feel good. Since God had shown me His unconditional love, I began to understand true love doesn't come from the hormones but from the heart. Real love wasn't dependent on feelings but was an act of the will. Oh, I still had crushes. Joanne Allen, the pastor's wife, was the first Christian woman that became my heart's model. I wonder if she noticed how awestruck I was. She set a good standard just by being who she was in Christ. There was a longing in my heart to find the right girl, but my search wasn't going too well. I guess the Lord figured there was no hurry since I was only sixteen.

When I began going to church, I met girls there—a lot of nice girls. Pat was one of the first Christian girls I dated. It didn't take too long, however, for me to realize we had different dreams for the future. She talked about the big house she hoped to have one day, but even then I thought about a missionary hut in a jungle.

"Do you ever think about being a missionary or pastor's wife?" I ventured.

Pat's reaction quickly ended that relationship.

Will I ever find a girl who shares my dreams? I wondered.

Charlie Roberts, an adult in our new church, took a personal interest in our family. On Sunday afternoons, he joined a group from another church and helped conduct open air evangelistic meetings in the streets and nearby housing projects. He invited my sisters and they were happy to go. They began telling me how exciting it was to lead others to the Lord as someone had led them to the Lord just a few months before that. It sounded interesting and I wanted to go with them, but I had a part-time job that included Sundays.

Roberta and Taffy told me about people they were meeting. Here were other teenagers who had similar interests and showed the same enthusiasm as we felt. We hadn't always seen that among the young people in our own church, because many of them had grown up in the church and took God for granted. They didn't have that flush of excitement new believers have.

The more my sisters talked, the more I wanted to belong to that group. I decided to find a job that would allow me time to get involved in Christian activities. That was one of the first conscious decisions I made to change my life for the sake of Christ. By the end of summer, I worked at Park's Pharmacy every evening after school and didn't work weekends.

I joined the open air group and began sharing my faith with others. I also made new friends.

One day I noticed a good-looking girl with dark hair and a quick smile. Her brown eyes twinkled as if she had a secret no one else knew. She listened intently when the leaders spoke and sang with enthusiasm. When she invited children to our meetings, her love for the Lord and the children was evident.

"Who's that?" I asked Taffy

"Her name is Kathy Hazen," she whispered, "and she's not going with anyone."

Slowly, Kathy and I built a friendship. We saw each other at open air activities once or twice a week. Kathy and I started making sure we were together Sunday afternoons when the group mobilized into teams, and our friends there began accepting us as a couple.

Though we had been together in group situations for several months, I was shy about asking Kathy for a real date. I wanted to ask her in person, but couldn't get opportunity and courage to coincide. I finally decided to ask her on the phone. I didn't want to call in front of my family, so I walked about one-half mile to Leonetti's Diner and called her from a pay phone.

All the way there, I chastised myself for not asking her in person. *I hate phones. Why didn't I ask her in person? I wonder who will answer. What should I say?*

I pulled the crumbled paper from my pocket and tried to read the wrinkled numbers. I dialed and it rang one, two… *Oh no, is that her mother?* I swallowed hard.

"Hello, is Kathy there?" I hoped my voice didn't sound as shaky as I felt.

"Just a minute." She was home.

I heard someone call out, "Kathy…telephone."

"Hello."

"Hi, uh, this is Dave Tucker—you know, from open air?" *Why did I say that? Of course she knows who I am. We've been together every Sunday afternoon.*

"Oh, hi," she replied.

"Well, uh, I just called because our high school's putting on *Brigadoon*, and I thought if you're not doing anything next Saturday… Well, would you like to go with me?"

When Kathy said "yes," I wasn't sure what to say next. I had concentrated so much on asking her, I hadn't thought about what to do if she said yes. We set a time, then I found out where she lived and said goodbye before she could change her mind.

I walked home feeling about two feet off the ground because she said yes. I knew something special was happening in my life, but it would be quite a while before I knew just how special.

That Saturday, I felt as physically awkward as I had felt tongue-tied on the phone. Mrs. Hazen opened the door and I mumbled, "hello." Obviously I was the only strange boy they were expecting that night, so she immediately called Kathy.

Kathy's family lived on the second floor of a two-family home. Relatively close quarters meant I got to meet everyone at once. Older brother, Bob, said a quick hello and left. Three-year-old sister, Debbie, took one look at me and hid behind Kathy's legs. She stayed close enough to know what was going on, but moved from hiding place to hiding place—behind people's legs, to the corner, to the wall, etc. Mr. Hazen's reserved demeanor was hard to read. I got the feeling Kathy was precious to him and I'd better treat her well—which I intended to do. Mrs. Hazen was more outgoing, talking and smiling often. Even as I took all this in, my focus was to get away with Kathy.

We attended *Brigadoon* that May 16, 1967. We enjoyed the play and felt comfortable conversing and learning more about each other. I finished the evening hoping we would have more times together.

A couple of weeks later our church youth group went to Palisades Amusement Park, and I asked Kathy to go with me. She hadn't dressed up, just shorts and a blouse, but I thought she looked beautiful. While we walked around, our hands "accidentally" touched and finally clasped. It's amazing the funny feelings a young man can get from holding hands.

Another youth group outing was a boat ride on the Hudson River. We sat on the upper deck watching heat lightning over the mountains. Thinking myself clever, I tried the old "put the arm on the back of the bench" thing. I thought I was looking so casual and subtle, but I guess I was rather obvious. Someone came along, pushed my arm onto her shoulder and said, "Oh, put your arm around her already!" I thought it was her brother, but later I learned her brother was preoccupied with his own love life and hadn't provided the nudge after all. Whoever it was, I owe him. I probably would have taken a long time to do this without that prompt.

That summer, Kathy went on a week's vacation with her family. A few days after she left, I was mowing the neighbor's lawn when Roberta waved a letter at me. I shut down the lawn mower and ran to get the letter. It was from Kathy. Happy to hear from her, I opened the envelope immediately. I read the letter twice, then folded it carefully and put it back in my pocket. I went back to mowing; but I kept thinking about the letter, and every few minutes I stopped the mower and read the letter again—because it was from "her."

Kathy was a virtuous Christian girl, refreshingly unlike the girls I had admired before becoming a believer. I valued our friendship. We continued to see each other and eventually began talking about a future of ministry together. Toward the end of our second college year we decided to marry. My head and heart agreed that she was "the one."

Friends recommended Alfred's Jewelers in Kathy's hometown, so we went there for a ring. Alfred's extraordinary concern for others showed as he walked us through the process, explaining what to look for in a diamond. Then he surprised me with the question, "For that money, would you like a bigger stone or a higher quality stone?"

We chose bigger. We had gone to him wanting and expecting just someone trustworthy who would give us an honest deal. Instead we found a friend who advised us and even gave us a discount. We put the ring in "lay away" and I began making regular payments.

I was working full-time that summer for the U.S. Post Office and made enough money to pay the ring off ahead of schedule, though Kathy didn't know it.

"Would you like to go into New York next weekend?" I asked.

"That would be fun. What would you like to do there?"

"I've never seen *Man of La Mancha*," I deadpanned.

By Kathy's reaction I knew I had chosen the right thing. An avid Spanish student in high school, she had seen the Broadway play about Don Quixote with her class. She had talked about the play until she raised my curiosity.

Back in New Jersey afterward, we sat in the park. Kathy laid her head on my shoulder and sighed, "I enjoyed seeing *Man of La Mancha* again. Thanks for thinking about that."

"We had a good day, didn't we? Something about Don Quixote and his impossible dream strikes a responsive chord in me. But we don't have anything to show anyone else about today."

Kathy looked at me with an expression that shouted, *Where are you going with this?*

Reaching in my pocket I said, "All day I've had something I've been waiting to give you so we can show everyone how we feel about each other." I knelt before her and watched her face flush with understanding.

"But you don't have the ring yet," she stammered.

Moonbeams played in her hair, and her eyes glistened with tears. I thought she had never looked so irresistible, and my heart felt as if it would burst with love. "Will you be my wife forever, Kathy?" I asked as I slipped the ring on her finger.

She whispered "yes" just as my lips touched hers. As we sealed our commitment with a tender kiss, I felt our hearts beating as one. We said our wedding vows on June 5, 1971, before our senior year of college. God still had much work to do in our lives; but we knew He loved us, we loved Him, and we loved each other.

CHAPTER TWO APPLICATION GUIDE

"But God shows and clearly proves His (own) love for us by the fact that while we were still sinners Christ, the Messiah, the Anointed One, died for us" Romans 5:8 (ANT).

God is love. His very nature is love. He loves us no matter what we do. What a liberating thought—and it gets even better. He is generous and shares His love with His children. If we allow the Holy Spirit to control our lives, He will produce this kind of love in us.

Though there are different kinds of love, the English language only allows one word. In America, we say we "love" pizza, we "love" to swim, we "love" our spouse, and we "love" our children. The love God gives is called "agape" in the Greek language. It is an unconditional love, without sexual connotations. It seeks, with pure motives, the best for another person. This love only comes from God. Our human nature is too selfish. "Dear friends, let us love one another, for love comes from God. Everyone who loves has been born of God and knows God. Whoever does not love does not know God, because God is love" I John 4:7-8 (NIV). If you don't see unconditional love developing in your life, talk with God (and a mature Christian who can help you place your trust in Christ) and be sure you have experienced spiritual rebirth.

Dave read Kathy's letter over and over because he loved her. Do you feel that desire to read God's Word over and over because you love Him? Reading God's Word helps us develop a loving relationship with Him. The more we get to know God, the more we will love Him.

Jesus gives an illustration, "I am the vine; you are the branches. If a man remains in me and I in him, he will bear much fruit; apart from me you can do nothing" John 15:5 (NIV). We only bear the fruit (characteristics) of God, when we cling to Him and let Him nourish our spiritual growth. Naturally, we will exhibit selfish character. Supernaturally, we can display God's love.

PONDER these Scriptures:

Jeremiah 31:3; I Corinthians 13:1-7; I John 4:7-21.

PRAISE God for His Love.

Think of several ways you have seen God show His love to you.

Think of some ways you have seen other Christians show God's love.

PEER into your heart.

Are you excited about reading God's love letter (the Bible)?

Are you showing God's unconditional love to others?

PRAYER

Loving Father, I praise You for Your unconditional, everlasting love. Thank You for giving Your love to me and sharing Your love through me. Please teach me new ways to put love into action. I pray for those who don't know about Your love. Please send a loving missionary to them. I pray in the Name of Jesus, Who showed us the ultimate expression of love. Amen

CHAPTER THREE

God Gives Support

"I'm glad you have that new job so you can join us on Sunday afternoons," Charlie said.

"Yeah," I answered, following my sisters into his car, "I think I'm glad too." On the thirty- minute drive to Hawthorne Gospel Church, I monopolized the conversation with questions. I didn't always like Charlie's answers, but I appreciated his willingness to explain his faith.

Charlie Roberts helped our pastor with the church youth group. Since we didn't have a car, Charlie picked us up for Sunday school and morning worship service, took us back home for dinner, then picked us up again for open air meetings. He frequently drove us to evening service and youth group activities as well.

When we arrived, the leader said, "Okay, we have twenty-five people today. Let's break into four groups." Each group went to a different area in Paterson, NJ. We confirmed responsibilities before we left. Within my group, Jorge said, "I brought my guitar." I found out later Jorge always had his guitar and nearly always led singing. Nancy was ready with a game which would lead to the story. Diane had prepared a story. As the new member my responsibilities included watching, helping keep order, and talking with kids who responded to the invitation.

We parked the car by an old blue truck with a bullet hole in the side window. Some of us started unpacking and a couple of kids stopped to see what was happening.

Nancy walked over to some girls jumping rope. "Hi. Want to come over and hear a story?"

Suddenly, a tall man flashing a diamond and wearing a big hat with a plume walked up to Charlie. Nearly touching noses the newcomer asked, "Hey, man, what's going on here? This is my neighborhood and anything happenin' here goes through me."

"We're here to tell people about Jesus," Charlie replied with just a slight tremble in his voice. "We're going to sing some songs and tell a Bible story. Would you like to stay?"

There was a minute of strained silence while the man thought. "Oh, okay. I can't stay, but you can. If anybody gives you any trouble, tell 'em Billy the Kid said it's okay."

"Jesus loves me, this I know…" Jorge walked up and down the street, playing his guitar and singing. A small crowd of children and a few curious adults followed him back.

By this time we had set up an easel full of blank paper and a flannelgraph board in front of the stores lining the street next to the housing project. We stood with our backs to the stores, while about a dozen children and a few adults filled the sidewalk.

Apart from my experience at "The Restless Ones," I had never heard a gospel message or invitation to receive Christ. I watched in awe as Diane told a simple story sticking flannel-backed figures on the board as visual aids.

"What color is sin?" she asked.

With little hesitation, the listening children answered what I was thinking: "Black."

"No," she said firmly. "The Bible never says sin is black. The only time the Bible gives sin a color, it's red."* Diane was speaking to African-Americans—Blacks in the language of that day.

This was a welcome revelation and caught their attention as she shared the gospel and gave an invitation to receive Jesus as Savior. Several hands went up, and members of our group rushed to talk and pray with those who responded. I wasn't sure what to do, but soon I was talking to Melrose, a boy of about eleven or twelve. "Mel, do you understand that Jesus died on the cross for your sins and mine?"

"Yes."

"Just talk to Him and ask Him to forgive your sins and save

---

*"Come now, and let us reason together, saith the LORD: though your sins be as **scarlet**, they shall be as white as snow; though they be **red** like crimson, they shall be as wool" (Isaiah 1:18 Emphasis added by the author)

you. I'll pray a sentence and you can repeat it, but you have to believe in your heart, okay?"

"Okay, I do."

We didn't have a good follow-up program, except through visiting the same locations frequently. But God is faithful to keep working in the hearts and lives of those who accept Him as Savior. I met Mel about four years later. He was attending a Sunday school class at Star of Hope Mission, and he was growing in the knowledge of Christ.

As God began preparing me for His service, my social life changed; and I became more of a leader instead of a follower. I had always liked to boss others around, but now I realized being a leader was more than that. I began to mature and care more about others.

I became a leader in the youth group and helped organize events during my senior year. In the late 1960s, church coffee houses became a popular outreach activity. Once a year our church converted the basement into a "coffee house" and invited young people from the area. Someone always shared a gospel message during this informal "seeker friendly" time.

One of our leaders had artistic talent and helped make invitations, which we passed out to the general public as well as church teens. We set up small round tables and covered them with red-checkered cloths. Instead of a coffee smell, a slight musty odor mixed with disinfectant fumes filled the air; but everyone seemed to enjoy this event.

We all joined in when Pastor Allen's seminary friend played the guitar and sang. We listened attentively to his sincere and enthusiastic message. Listening to him and observing his manner, I thought serving the Lord must be a great privilege.

Later that night I walked into our house and shouted, "I'm going to be a preacher!"

That brought my mother running. "What did you say?"

Suddenly the realization of what I'd said hit me, and I became very serious. In awe I repeated, "I'm going to be a preacher."

"Why do you say that, Dave?"

Taking a deep breath, I looked directly at my mother. "I don't know why. I just know I have to do this. Something happened tonight at the coffee house."

I'm not sure if what happened that night was because of anything the speaker said. It was more what he did and how he did it. He expressed love and joy, and I coveted that. I came away from that evening with an overwhelming conviction that I should be in full-time Christian work. I didn't know what, where, when, or how—but God did.

The Lord was fostering spiritual growth in my sisters, too. From our pastor's wife, they heard about a Christian group for teenagers. It was called Hi BA, which stood for High School Born Againers, formally known as High School Evangelism, Inc. Taffy and Roberta wanted to reach their friends with the gospel, and Hi BA seemed like a good tool for growth and outreach. They found an address and sent a letter asking, "Can we help start a Hi BA club at our school?"

They learned such a club already existed in our area, drawing kids from several schools including ours. The club met each Thursday after school, and we joined immediately.

One week our HI BA club leader announced that Vera Kelly would speak about her work in Alaska. This was the first time I heard a missionary talk. We saw slides of beautiful scenery, and Vera's radiant joy was evident. Vera worked with a group known then as Central Alaska Mission, which a few years later merged into SEND International. Missions attracted me immediately; but little did I know that thirty years later I would be recruitment director for SEND International, actually sending new missionaries to carry on the work Vera introduced me to that night.

God was training us through many avenues and soon gave us a new opportunity.

"An abandoned church building in New York is available," Pete Everett, our open air leader, shared one Sunday afternoon. "It's an old run-down building with steep steps leading up to one large room. It needs a lot of work; but there are no other churches in the area, and the former pastor said we could use it for our outreach ministry."

Raised hands and dozens of questions followed this announcement.

"I don't know the answers to all your questions, but we're going to meet here at 9:00 a.m. next Saturday, and you can see the building for yourself."

Delighted, we met and enthusiastically worked hard cleaning and repairing "our building." After working every Saturday for two months, we looked around the freshly mowed lawn and weedless flower beds, the clean rectangular room with a cross behind the pulpit, the mended benches, and the polished piano. We felt the heat from the repaired furnace and smelled the cleaner and furniture polish. We prayed, "Thank You, Lord for giving us this building where we can share Your good news with others."

Finally, we held our first meeting on a Sunday afternoon. We had prepared special invitations and distributed them throughout the neighborhood. We were able to get Art Williams, the head of Open Air Campaigners, to speak. Many of our group participated by leading songs or giving testimonies. It was a wonderful day culminating many months of preparation. Several people responded to the gospel message, and we were on cloud nine.

The next week, though, Mr. Everett told us our first meeting had been our last. When the family that owned the building saw what was happening, they took control of the church and told our group there wasn't a place for us there after all. We were all disheartened. No, we were outright angry. It seemed unfair. We had worked so hard to put the church back in operation. Then, after we did the major work, someone else took over what we thought would be the easy—the fun—part. In retrospect, I realize we could have run that church only as an evangelistic preaching point, not as a true church. We didn't have the spiritual maturity to provide effective leadership. On a more positive note, this time of seeing God work through our group bonded us together and created a true one-body synergy that is rare and precious.

God used this period of time to develop our spiritual gifts, too. We enjoyed exercising these gifts and looked for opportunities. Charlie Roberts often volunteered at Good Shepherd Rescue Mission, so it seemed natural that my sisters and I started helping there.

"Dave, how would you like to preach at Good Shepherd next month?" Charlie looked at me from the corner of his eye then turned his attention back to the road. I wondered, *Does he know during his sermon tonight I was daydreaming about what I would say if given the chance?*

Trying to sound calm I replied, "I think I'd like to give it a try."

I began my first public sermon, "Tonight we're going to visit hell." My audience was a group of about twenty-five men, most of whom we could describe as "street people." Some were there because they needed a meal and a place to sleep. Some had already experienced God's love and this was the only church they knew.

Maybe I can scare them into heaven by talking about hell, I thought while searching for a topic. Not knowing how to prepare a sermon, I had gone through a concordance and found various descriptions of hell or eternal punishment. Now I read these descriptions, one after another, for fifteen to twenty minutes.

I concluded, "But you don't have to settle for hell. God has a better offer, and I'm here tonight to tell you about it." Then I gave the same invitation to which I had responded—the only invitation I knew. "Who would like to accept God's offer of salvation through Jesus Christ?"

Several men raised their hands and stayed around to ask questions and pray. God showed me what He could do with a little knowledge, a lot of enthusiasm, and a willing spirit.

My immediate reaction was relief that my speaking engagement was over. But I felt good about what I had done as Charlie, Taffy, and Roberta congratulated me. I looked forward to more chances to serve God through speaking.

While I was excited about growing spiritually, I was putting forth as little effort as possible academically. Teachers said, "Dave, you could do so much better if only you'd apply yourself."

Though I had some direction because I knew I wanted to serve God, I didn't know how to get where I wanted to go. Instead of looking to God for guidance, I depended on my own understanding. No doubt I would have to go to seminary, which meant getting a college degree first. So I enrolled in Rutgers University as a commuting student and thought I would spend the next four years "getting by" while waiting for seminary.

College studies were more intense than I had anticipated and demanded my concentration. Left-wing political activism was generating an anti-religious feeling on campus, and I felt out of place. There must have been other believers there, but I never found them. It wasn't long before I wondered if I had made the right decision.

One day I stopped in the hallway with my hand on a doorknob and asked myself aloud, "Why am I here?" I had no answer. I turned around, walked to my car, and drove away.

I was embarrassed to tell my family and friends I had quit college. This was the first major failure I had experienced. For several weeks I went through the routine of leaving home in the morning and returning in the afternoon. I spent a lot of time in libraries and parks, hiding my failure from my family. However, this also provided time for talking with God about my future. Parks were good. There I could walk, think, and pray aloud. "Lord, where did I go wrong? This seemed like a logical thing to do. Why didn't you tell me it would turn out this way?"

I remembered a similar situation when I asked the same question: "Mom, you knew this would turn out this way. Why didn't you warn me?"

It seemed to me, her answer then was God's answer now: "Would you have listened? I had to let you fail so you would be ready to take my advice. Are you ready to start listening?"

Yes, I was ready.

A few days later I went to my sisters' room to talk. "May I close the door, girls? I have something to tell you." I had already told my mother, so this was the next step. My younger sisters and I had developed a special bond since we had become Christians.

"I dropped out of college. I blew it."

Before they could comment, I rushed ahead knowing if I didn't say everything at once, I might not get it out at all. "I was right about what God wants me to do. I thought I could figure out how to do it on my own, but I found out the hard way that I can't. Now that I'm listening to Him, I think He wants me to go to Northeastern Bible College."

"We know that," Taffy and Roberta replied together. Seeing my stunned look, Taffy continued for both of them, "We always thought you should go to Northeastern, but we knew you probably wouldn't listen to us. We've been praying since last year that God would show you."

"That's right," Roberta chimed in, "You didn't tell us anything new tonight. You just told us how God answered our prayers."

I told my father last. We had a good talk; and he agreed to pay for my schooling.

Finally in place at Northeastern Bible College a few months later, I had a purpose for learning. I knew I was where God wanted me to prepare for serving Him. I began to excel and found myself on the dean's list.

Now that I was following, God was ready to lead me to the next step.

"Who's in chapel today?" John called as he caught up to me after class. A daily chapel service was part of the schedule at Northeastern Bible College. Speakers included faculty, area pastors, and missionaries on home leave.

"Not sure," I called back. "The bulletin board listed someone from Unevangelized Fields Mission, but I think he works in the office. I'd rather hear a missionary from the field."

"Hey, look at all this stuff," I pointed John to the missionary display in the chapel lobby. "Here's a brochure about where they work."

"I'd leave that alone," cautioned John. "You might find yourself called to the jungle."

"I can't say that I'd mind," I replied, my hands fixed on one particular piece of paper. "Look at this, John. This is a list of their fields. I recognize all of the countries except this one—West Irian." As I read on, my grip on the paper tightened. "Hey! This place is part of New Guinea. There are hundreds of tribes there with no gospel witness. Each one has its own language. Some of these tribes practice cannibalism and headhunting. This mission is looking for general missionaries who can live in a stone-age civilization, learn the language, and start churches."

John pulled on my sleeve. "Come on, Dave, let's get into our seats. What kind of person would want to live in a place like that anyway?"

I smiled to myself. *What kind of person would go to West Irian? Someone who has an adventurous outlook; someone who is not satisfied doing what has been done before; someone who wants a challenge; someone who wants to do something exciting for Christ. Me!*

Even though this sounded like the most exciting invitation I'd ever received, I kept this idea to myself for a few weeks, wondering if it was from the Lord or if it was born in my own adventurous spirit. Then something very strange began happening. I picked up a news magazine and found a story on West Irian. Two weeks before I would not have recognized the name; now I devoured the article. Later browsing through an old *National Geographic*, I saw a feature on the Asmat tribe of West Irian. A week later another missionary came to chapel to speak about—you guessed it—West Irian. It seemed Someone was turning my attention toward West Irian.

Then came an event that sealed my commitment. Listening to the radio one day in September of 1968, I heard a news report about two missionaries who had been killed by tribespeople in West Irian. From what I could gather, Stan Dale and Phil Masters, missionaries working with Regions Beyond Missionary Union in West Irian, were God's latest martyrs. They had been struck down by arrows from the Yali people whom they were trying to reach for Christ.

Bending over that radio trying to catch every word, something clicked inside me. It was as if a lighted sign appeared before my eyes saying, "Pay attention, Dave. This is your invitation."

I dropped to my knees. "Lord, if You will let me, I'll go to West Irian and take the place of one of these men."

I finally knew *what* I would do and *where* I would do it. I still wondered *when* and *how*, but God would show me in His time.

At the beginning of our senior year, Kathy and I were married and moving together toward service in West Irian. We wanted to work with an established missionary organization and had narrowed our choice to three non-denominational missions. Each did evangelism and church planting in West Irian, now renamed Irian Jaya. All were good organizations. We had developed friendships with missionaries within all three. How could we choose?

"Kathy, find a table so I can set this stuff down." My arms full of brochures, doctrinal statements, and policy manuals, I followed her into the snack shop. This was the night of decision.

We sorted the papers into three piles: Unevangelized Field Mission, The Evangelical Alliance Mission, and the Regions Beyond Missionary Union. "Dave, hand me that doctrinal statement," Kathy said. "Let's start comparing these missions point by point."

And that's what we did. We read each paper again—not looking for the best mission agency, but looking for the best fit between a mission and our personalities and our vision.

"Choices like this aren't easy." By this time I was speaking to many fellow students who had gathered around our table to observe our decision-making process. "But this is it, isn't it, Kak?" I put my hand on an application form.

"That's the one," she agreed. We waited for trumpets to play or angels to sing, but we only heard dishes rattling and people chattering. Yet, we knew in our hearts God was guiding us to apply to the Regions Beyond Missionary Union (RBMU).

In August of the next year we went to the RBMU candidate school in Philadelphia. This would be the final stage of our application. There we would meet the rest of the mission staff, be interviewed by the Council members, and get our assignment. Considering the way God had led so far, I never doubted our acceptance into the RBMU family of missionaries.

As icing on the cake, we met a new circle of friends. The mission staff became our friends and partners, as well as about fifteen other candidates looking to become RBMU missionaries. Some would be our future coworkers in Irian Jaya. Others were heading for places like Borneo, Peru, and the Congo. We had a common interest, and we especially enjoyed talking about pioneer missionaries. Several had given the ultimate sacrifice for Christ, like Phil Masters and Stan Dale, whose martyrdom had played a crucial part in God's leading me to Irian Jaya. They had blazed the trail and left a model for us.

I was young, eager, enthusiastic, and totally lacking in patience. I was ready to board the next plane leaving for Irian Jaya.

"David," Joe said in his impressive bass voice. Joseph F. Conley was U.S. Executive Director for the Regions Beyond Missionary Union. He stood tall and looked serious; I turned my full attention on him. Joe used a single syllable word only when a longer one didn't fit, and with him this seemed natural. "The U.S. Council has discerned the hand of God on you and Kathy. They see that you are young, eager, and enthusiastic."

I was feeling pretty good at that point.

"They also note that you lack patience and seasoning. With this in mind, they would like you to participate in an internship program to furnish you with some meaningful experience under appropriate tutelage. Don't misconstrue this and perceive it as an interruption in your plans. Rather this is an opportunity to hone your not-insignificant skills before going overseas."

So two weeks later, Kathy and I were pulling a U-Haul trailer along Interstate 80, heading toward Michigan. We were going as interns to the First Baptist Church in Imlay City, a small town about fifty miles north of Detroit. For the next nine months we would spend three of every four weeks working at a variety of tasks around the church. Pastor Millard Heron guided us through participating in almost all ministry aspects of a small local church. This included everything from visiting church members to preparing the weekly bulletin on a mimeograph machine, and fixing the machine when it broke.

Pastor Heron let me speak the two Sundays he was on vacation. The first Sunday I concentrated so much on my message, I forgot to take the offering.

We spent each fourth week at Missionary Internship (M.I.) in Farmington, a Detroit suburb. The M.I. staff all had significant missionary experience. They were there to pass along the wisdom they had gained through experience to us—the next generation of God's missionaries.

I began that year with a bad attitude. I really didn't think internship was necessary. We had trained enough. Despite what Joe Conley thought, it would only delay our agenda. Yet, God knew how much we would grow during these nine months. Though we went to minister, we were surprised how much the people ministered to us. They saw us as part of their contribution to missions. They patiently worked to prepare "the kids" for effective ministry. This church had a vision and a tremendous record for preparing and sending missionaries. These wise Christians became our friends. They encouraged me to step out in faith and let me learn by experience. They forgave my mistakes and gently corrected me with love.

Returning home to New Jersey after our internship, Kathy and I plunged into what we saw as the final leg of our journey to Irian Jaya. Few new missionaries look forward to this time, commonly referred to as *deputation* or *support discovery*. We were not exceptions. Deputation usually involves contacting churches and asking them to make a monthly financial commitment. Missionaries also encourage the church to support them emotionally through communication and spiritually through prayer. This can be a humbling and fearful experience.

We had a couple of advantages. First was a strong missions-minded home church. Hawthorne Gospel Church quickly committed itself to providing one-third of our financial needs.

Our second advantage takes some explanation. During our missionary internship, we met a missionary who served in Irian Jaya. Don and Carol Richardson ministered with RBMU to the Sawi people.

The Sawi were both cannibals and headhunters. They idealized treachery. To accommodate the lack of trust, they had developed the custom of giving a living child as a token of peace and trust between two warring factions which wanted to stop fighting. As long as the child lived, the two sides could not fight. This was the *tarop tim*, or, as Don later popularized the concept, the *peace child*. Don and Carol showed the Sawi how this peace child custom paralleled what God did in giving His Son, Jesus Christ as a peace child between Himself and mankind. Because Jesus has eternal life, whoever receives God's Peace Child has eternal peace.

Don wrote a book entitled, *Peace Child*, in which he described the tremendous positive effect this redemptive analogy had for the Sawi people. Just as Kathy and I were beginning deputation, *Peace Child* was made into a short film. RBMU had one copy of the film, and could show it only if a mission representative were present. They didn't have enough office staff to send around the country to all the groups requesting the film, so they made Kathy and me the official representatives. *Peace Child* gave us an entrance into many churches and opportunities to present our own vision of working with one of the Sawi's neighboring tribes.[1]

With these two advantages, the Lord moved us through the major milestones of deputation. I was able to quit my job and concentrate on full-time support discovery.

Even though our first child, Gwen, was born during this time, we lacked for nothing we really needed. Within six months we had full support. We applied for a visa that usually took three months to process. Instead the visa came in one month, and we moved ahead according to God's timing.

On April 23, 1975, the church parking lot filled with well-wishers. Pastor Jim Richmond pulled up in the "old green monster," as we called our church bus. The bus full of family and friends led several cars across the George Washington Bridge to New York's J.F.K. Airport where the church choir sang God's blessings on us.

We were really on our way to Irian Jaya. God had prepared us financially, physically, intellectually, emotionally, and spiritually for His work. He had given generously to Christians, and some of them had shared generously with us. Through them, God had provided all we needed.

---

1. *Peace Child*, Don Richardson, Glendale, CA, Regal Books, 1976

CHAPTER THREE APPLICATION GUIDE

"And my God will liberally supply (fill to the full) your every need according to His riches in glory in Christ Jesus" Philippians 4:19 (ANT).

God is rich. There is nothing He can't give us, but He chooses what gifts are best for us. Often, we think of riches as just material goods, such as money, houses, cars, boats, jewelry, or toys, but God wants the incorruptible as our priorities. (Read Matthew 6:19-21.)

God has every resource we need, and He is more than willing to share with us. We can develop our faith by focusing on His provision instead of our problems. The more we read the Bible and get to know God, the more we will learn to lean on Him.

NEED	SCRIPTURE	FOCUS
Material needs	Philippians 4:19	God's sufficiency
Weakness	Ephesians 3:20-21	God's strength
Confusion	Romans 11:33-34	God's wisdom
Fear	Isaiah 26:3-4	God's peace
Loneliness	Psalm 73:23-24	God's presence

Changing our focus (mental picture) from "I am poor" to "God is rich" or "I am weak" to "God is strong" or "I am confused" to "God is wise" influences our feelings and performance tremendously. Instead of whining to God about our needs, let's try praising Him for His resources.

God gives generously, and those who follow Him give generously. People generously shared their time and resources to love, teach, disciple, train, educate, encourage, and support the Tuckers. God will give us opportunities to share, too, if we keep our hearts, minds, eyes, and pockets open.

PONDER these Scriptures:

Matthew 6:19-21, 10:8; Acts 2:43-47; Ephesians 3:14-21.

PRAISE Jesus for His willingness to leave glory and riches to come to earth.

Consider what Jesus left in heaven.

Consider what Jesus came to on earth.

PEER into your heart.

When you pray, do you focus on your problems or God's provisions?

Do you trust God to supply all your needs?

PRAYER

All Sufficient Father, I praise You for Your riches in glory. Thank You for reserving incorruptible riches as an inheritance for me. I pray for missionaries who have left the comforts of home for Your sake. Please help me be willing to follow wherever You lead me. Please help me to follow Jesus' example by being a servant and sharing generously with others as I go about my daily life. Help me to value what is lasting. Help me wisely prioritize the temporary things of this earthly life. Amen.

CHAPTER FOUR

God Gives Vision

"Irian Jaya, here we come," I exclaimed as the plane lifted off the tropical island of Biak.

"Finally, the last leg of the trip." Kathy squeezed my hand and smiled. "Just two more hours, and we'll be there."

Though excitement overcame our weariness, Gwen held her head and began to whimper. Five days of travel was taking its toll on our little daughter. So far we had come across the Atlantic Ocean, through Europe and Asia, and now we were in the South Pacific.

As Kathy soothed Gwen, I looked out the window of our DC3 propeller-driven plane and saw several small islands. *What islands were these?* I had studied the map of this area often, yet there were many islands I couldn't identify. I rested my head on the back of the seat and closed my eyes, while my mind wandered back to many questions I had answered, "I don't know. Let me get back to you."

Ken Brown was a close friend who had often asked me questions I couldn't answer. One day he said, "Dave, you talk about going to Indonesia and you talk about going to Irian Jaya. Are they the same?"

"Ken, I'm glad you finally asked me a question I can answer." Being a history buff, I loved to discuss things I had learned.

"Indonesia is the name of the country and Irian Jaya is a fairly new province in that country. It is southeast of mainland

Asia and northwest of Australia. Indonesia includes 13,700 islands and about half are inhabited. One of the larger islands is now divided into Irian Jaya, part of the Indonesian government, and Papua New Guinea, an independent nation."

"I didn't realize Indonesia included so many islands," Ken said. "Do you know how the island of New Guinea separated into two different governments?"

"For years the island of New Guinea was divided between the Germans and British who colonized the eastern half, and the Dutch who colonized the western half and called it West Irian. During World War II, the Japanese took over Indonesia and the island.

"The Japanese talked about 'Asia for the Asians,' and this made them many friends among people who had been dominated by European powers. Also, the Indonesians had a tradition passed down for hundreds of years that tall, pale-skinned people would dominate them. The story said short, yellow-skinned people would push away the pale-skinned people; and Indonesia would find unity and freedom.

"I don't know if the Japanese knew about this tradition or not, but when they realized they were losing the war, they declared Indonesia an independent nation before leaving it.

"After the war, the Dutch attempted to take back areas they had controlled, but the Indonesians wanted to keep their independence, and there was a bloody civil war which lasted several years. The hatred continues to divide many still today.

"The island of New Guinea was very different culturally than the rest of Indonesia, which caused even more conflict. West Irian remained under Dutch auspices, but the Indonesians tried to claim it also. In the early 1960s, the United Nations interceded and the people of West Irian voted on whether to remain under Dutch rule, become a separate country, or become Indonesian. They became part of Indonesia. Later West Irian changed its name to Irian Jaya (Glorious Irian)."

"I wonder where RBMU will assign us to work?" Kathy's question broke my reverie.

"We'll soon know," I answered before my thoughts moved to people groups in various areas and the stories I had heard about missionaries who worked with them.

Will we minister among the Dani tribe? I wondered. It was natural for me to think of the Dani first since RBMU missionaries had worked with them most. In fact, when we had landed in Biak and I saw my first Irianese tribesman, I had wondered aloud if he were a Dani. A high school student returning to his missionary family had explained there were over two hundred different tribal groups in Irian Jaya, each with their own location and language.

Some of the stories I had heard about the Dani surfaced in my mind. I remembered hearing how missionary, Jerry Rose, attended a Dani funeral and watched in horror as chanting mourners picked up huge rocks and beat their own heads until blood gushed over their bodies. They carried the dead warrior to a large funeral pyre and laid the corpse's weapons and headdress next to it. As a flaming torch ignited the wood, the mourners continued chanting.

To express sorrow, some Dani women and girls chopped off their fingers with stone axes. Since boys needed their fingers for pulling bowstrings, they donated the upper portions of their ears. The older men roasted the ear parts and fingers and passed them around to the mourning relatives, who ate them.

Missionaries also heard of Danis feasting on victims after battles. Tom Bozeman told this story: "The Danis around Hetigima told me that there was hardly a person in our area that had not tasted human flesh at one time or another. Yet, it's funny when you talk to the Danis on our side of the Baliem. They say, 'Oh, no, we don't eat people; they do it on the other side of the river.' But when you question the residents of the opposite side of the valley, they deny the charge and accuse the Danis in our area."[2]

The Dani tribe now had many believers. John and Helen Dekker from RBMU had been working with this group since 1960, and they had seen God changing lives radically . The Danis were sending their own missionaries to help reach other tribes in Irian Jaya. Don Richardson was using some of these Dani evangelists in his outreach among the Sawi. I envisioned God using Kathy and me in a dramatic ministry such as this, yet looking at my wife and child made me happy it wasn't as dangerous to minister in Irian Jaya now.

Whichever tribe we minister among, I'm thankful for those missionaries who went before us and paved the way. Thinking

[2] *Cannibal Valley*, Russell T. Hitt, 1962, Christian Publications, Harrisburg, PA.

about how God had worked in their lives and through their lives encouraged me.

I thought about Einar Mickelson who came to the Wissel Lakes area shortly after World War II ended. He got some people from the Kapauku tribe to help him build a two-room bamboo house. Others from the tribe weren't happy with them being there, however, and at dusk a group of Kapaukus with crude weapons surrounded his house.

Mickelson dropped to his knees and spent the night praying earnestly. In the morning the warriors were gone, and Mickelson went about his Father's business.

At that time, brothers or uncles often sold little girls when they reached the age of ten or so. One Kapauku girl named Tebaimabijuwua begged for help from missionary Darlene Rose, who was her teacher. The girl's big brother had sold her to an older man for some cowrie shells. She tried to hide, but the two men found her and the brother shot her with arrows. The child dashed through the missionary's door with blood streaming down her shoulder; and her brother followed, threatening to kill her.

Darlene sent for the chieftain of the village, then prayed ardently.

The girl's brother had already accepted the cowrie shells; and the chieftain, trying to find a compromise, suggested the couple marry and both attend school. Tebaimabijuwua broke into tears while a bystander taunted her. Darlene tried to comfort the child, and could hold back her own tears no longer."

The Lord touched the chieftain's heart and he responded, "Mama's crying because she loves and pities one of her schoolgirls. If she teaches them, she may say what they do." [3]

This ruling contradicted centuries of looking at women and children as possessions only. It provided a vision of hope in a world full of injustice and cruelty.

My ears begin to fill with pressure. Were we descending already? I looked out the window and saw the wings tip. Soon we felt the slight jar of wheels touching the runway. Hot, heavy air settled over us as the door opened. It was April 29, 1975, when we landed at Sentani airport near Jayapura, Irian Jaya's capital city. Though it was only about ten o'clock in the morning the

---

[3] Ibid.

temperature must have been above ninety degrees, with humidity to match.

Carrying Gwen and several small bags, we bumped our way through the aisle and down the steps.

"Look, Gwen," I turned her in my arms so she could see the edge of the airport. "Those are coconut trees. And look above the trees. See the parrots flying?"

Kathy pointed in another direction. "Those people are walking across the runway like it's one of their regular pathways." We found out later it was.

"Welcome to Irian Jaya, Kathy and Dave," a voice boomed across the tarmac. Field Chairman David Martin had walked from the terminal to greet us. A chorus of "hello," and "welcome" sounded from the entrance to the terminal building. Most of the other RBMU missionaries based in Sentani had come to the airport. We appreciated the great reception.

That evening David and his wife Margy hosted a welcome party in their home at the Bible school campus. New names, faces, sights, smells, impressions, and information swam in our heads. Just when we thought we couldn't take in any more, David took us into his office to give us a schedule for the next several months.

"Dave and Kathy, eventually you'll have to learn at least two languages. The second will be the tribal language to which you'll be assigned. Before that you should be fluent in Indonesian, the national language. Most tribes have someone who can speak Indonesian because it is the trade language. We'd like to get you involved in Indonesian study as soon as possible."

David paused. "There is a snag."

We leaned forward; he had our full attention.

"We used to have a good language course here in Irian Jaya. But that ended a few months ago. We had hoped to place you in a course on another island, but they will not be ready for students until a year from now."

"So what do we do now?" I broke in.

"Several other missions here have pooled resources with us to hold a one-month Indonesian refresher course for our missionaries." David saw the surprised look on my face and hurried on.

"You were asked to bring along some Indonesian study books. Do you have these in your luggage?"

Kathy and I nodded.

"Good. I'm going to start you two working with a tutor and using those books. You have a month before the course begins. If you really work at it, I'm sure you can fit in."

Two days later we heard a voice at the door calling, "knock, knock." Missionary Bill Rosenberger flew through the door with his Indonesian language book in hand. Bill was short and round and always moving. Most of his friends called him Rosie.

"You guys can't study this on your own. I'm not the best Indonesian speaker, but I'm available. How about if I spend a couple of hours with you each day?"

We found out Rosie wasn't the most grammatically correct Indonesian speaker, but he was fluent. He had learned on the job, helping local workmen construct the building from which he ran Regions Press. Rosie taught us the working man's language, and that helped us immensely.

The weekend before formal classes began, I learned classes would be on three levels—beginning, intermediate, and advanced. I thought missionaries who had been working there for several years would be at the advanced level, but many had focused on learning their tribal language until now.

I heard that the intermediate class would begin with chapter four of the language book Kathy and I had been using. Since we were already on chapter three, I convinced myself this would be a great opportunity to impress my fellow missionaries. I only needed to memorize one hundred more vocabulary words to reach chapter four, and I had a whole weekend to do it.

I quickly learned that memorizing words didn't mean I could use them correctly. By jumping into the intermediate level, I had bypassed the necessary practice, practice, practice. If I had stayed with the beginners, I might have impressed my fellow missionaries; instead I struggled through the intermediate class. My pride suffered as God began teaching me that rushing ahead doesn't always produce good results.

During this time we received our long-term assignment—the village of Kawem, among the Kayagar people in Irian Jaya's southern lowlands. A RBMU missionary couple, John and Glenna, had been working at Kawem for over ten years. Now they were leaving the field for good.

We met John as he was passing through Sentani on his way to the states. His wife and two of their four children had already left Kawem. When he learned I was his replacement, he declared, "The Kayagar had their chance. I poured many years into them, and they didn't respond to the gospel. We should use our limited resources where they bring the most return. We shouldn't waste any more time on the Kayagar."

"But," I protested, "that sounds so harsh. If it's that bad, why are we even going there?"

"RBMU thinks we should try again. I don't. I've had it with the Kayagar. If you want my advice, you'll stay away from Kawem. You can do what you want, but I'm leaving."

Kathy verbalized some of the same questions I had. "What do we do now? Is he right? Should we go to Kawem if the people there have rejected Christ?" This started a conversation between us which lasted several days.

I didn't have any answers and was willing to admit it. "I don't know, Kak. We're not as experienced as John, and I might be naive; but I can't believe our leadership would give us this assignment if the situation is as bad as he says."

We talked to other missionaries and found out John was a very conservative man with high standards. Since most people's standards are based on culture, it was very difficult for him to reach across cultural lines. His personality was so different from Kayagar tribal culture that they never felt comfortable together.

"Maybe," Kathy summed up a couple of days later, "the Kayagar people had more of a problem with the missionary than with the gospel. If that's the case, we certainly need to try something new in Kawem to help them see beyond the missionary—beyond us—to Christ Himself."

We determined to give them that chance.

Shortly after that I chatted with one of the Mission Aviation Fellowship (MAF) pilots. When I told him we were going to Kawem, he said, "Don't go there. Nobody wants to go there. You certainly don't want to go. Just tell them you won't go and you want another assignment." He had lived in that area while flying a floatplane and he knew how bad the weather and living conditions were. He also knew the people in the south coast were much less responsive to the gospel than the people in the highlands. Within a year, workers in the highlands saw thousands receive Christ and several churches established. Entire tribes came to Christ. While in the south coast missionaries working with the Sawi, Autohoim, Kayagar, or Asmat, often reaped a handful of believers during several years.

People shared all kinds of warnings. One said, "Watch out for crocodiles. One day a teacher, Guru Rumbiak, walked along the riverside in Pirimapun. His son walked behind him, stopping to pick up small pieces of shell. Movement in the water must have attracted the toddler, and he wandered closer to the river. Suddenly, a salt-water crocodile came halfway on shore, lunged at the boy, and disappeared with a quick slap of his tail. Guru Rumbiak turned and saw his son in the crocodile's mouth. He screamed and ran as fast as he could, but he was too late. He fell on the crushed shells covering the riverside, weeping and repeating, 'I'll never see my baby again; never feel his little hand grasp mine; never hear his voice calling me *Bapa* (Daddy).'"

It was a small consolation to know only fresh-water crocodiles lived near Kawem. They are less aggressive, but I didn't really want to meet any crocodiles in my yard. We vowed to keep our little Gwen close at all times.

With all the weird advice we received about Kawem, we didn't know what to expect, how to act toward the people, or how the people would receive us.

One of the RBMU missionaries said, "Build a big fence around your yard with one gate. Put a big dog by that gate so the people don't bother you."

We felt confused. How could we get close to the people and still protect ourselves from harm? We determined we couldn't. We committed ourselves to the Kayagar and to establishing close relationships with them. God had given us the vision to reach them. He would protect us.

There was one more step to take before moving to Kawem. It was a two-week orientation on the South Coast. John and Esther Mills were veteran missionaries in Kamur village where the Sawi people lived, only one river north of our goal. John and Esther would help us adjust to life in the lowlands.

Looking down from the floatplane at the winding Kronkel River, I thought about Don and Carol Richardson's pioneering move into Kamur years earlier. They had been the first outsiders to live and minister among the Sawi tribe. They had brought a young child with them, too. At that time the Sawi and most surrounding tribes were practicing headhunters and cannibals. God had protected the Richardsons; we were confident He would protect us, too.

I gazed at Gwen. She rarely sat so still. Her eyes moved back and forth from one window to another. What did she think about these new surroundings? The vibrations of the small plane mesmerized her until she finally drifted off to sleep.

I looked around the unfamiliar environment. Would we ever feel at home here? Steaming hot rain forest covered most of the terrain with tall trees stretching high to reach the sun, sago palms vying for ground, and vines entangling anything within their reach. Because of the heat and humidity, we always felt damp—and so did everything around us.

When we got to Kamur, the Mills greeted us warmly and gave us a tour of the village. "I'm sorry our furlough is coming just when you are arriving," John Mills said. "We'll just get to know you by the time we leave for Canada and you move to Kawem. At least we can help you settle into life in these lowlands."

They introduced us to Ken and Mary Studd from Australia, who would fill in during the Mills' furlough. Ken and Mary had lived in Irian Jaya a year. They had learned basic Indonesian and were beginning to study the Sawi language.

Gwen charmed them all; everyone she met was her friend. Her curiosity and outgoing personality also made her reach toward everything new. We watched carefully for poisonous snakes and other dangers, but malaria we couldn't avoid. About three weeks after we got to Kamur, Gwen became feverish. When her temperature shot up to one-hundred-five degrees, we started her on malaria medication.

What have we done bringing this vulnerable baby into this culture? We were not only battling sickness, we were battling spiritual forces. Whenever doubts came, we cried out to God and His Holy Spirit comforted and encouraged us. He also gave us a vision for helping the Kayagar, who battled sickness and spiritual forces with no hope.

Then Ken and his daughter, Elizabeth, came down with hepatitis. This highly infectious disease had been working its way through the missionary community for some months. Potentially lethal, hepatitis was fairly easy to treat, but the treatment required weeks of total bed rest. As soon as the Mills went north and we went south, the work of seven people would fall on Mary and her teenage son, Iain. After talking things over with the Studds and Mills, we asked our field leadership if we could stay until Ken recuperated. Our two-week orientation turned into a three-month exposure to village life.

Staying at Kamur for that extended time was one of the best training experiences we could have had. We saw an established mission station in operation, we grew more used to the climate, and we began ministering alongside others who could help us when we made mistakes.

John Mills did a lot of thinking but often didn't share his thoughts until they became a plan. "Esther and I are leaving in two weeks, Dave. Why don't I organize a canoe trip next week to take you over to Kawem and introduce you to the people there? We'll stay a couple of nights and visit some other Kayagar villages along the way."

I tried not to show my excitement, but inside I was shouting, *Finally, I'll get to see where Kathy and I might spend the rest of our lives!*

CHAPTER FOUR APPLICATION GUIDE

"...I am sending you to them to open their eyes and turn them from darkness to light, and from the power of Satan to God, so that they may receive forgiveness of sins and a place among those who are sanctified by faith in me" Acts 26:17b-18 (NIV).

God gives spiritual vision. Without His intervention we don't see beyond ourselves, and we never see the spiritual needs of others.

God gave Dave and Kathy, along with many other missionaries, a vision of learning the culture and then sharing the true gospel of Christ so people in that culture could understand. Once people accept Christ as Savior and learn what God says in the Bible, the Holy Spirit convicts the believers of sin and their lives change. The Kayagar people gained physically, emotionally, and spiritually because the Tuckers acted on the vision God gave them.

Dave and Kathy caught God's vision for reaching out and drawing others into His family. God's family includes many diverse people, and we can celebrate the differences instead of trying to push everyone into the same mold. Look at the diversity God created in the plant and animal world. God also created people as individuals, and each one influences a certain group of people and has unique opportunities for sharing God's strategy of salvation.

Mr. Murthi, an Indian evangelist, once said, "Do not bring us the Gospel as a potted plant. Bring us the seed of the Gospel and plant it in our soil"

God blesses us with the vision of blessing others. God's plan is to draw people from every nation and tribe into His Circle of Blessing.

PONDER these Scriptures:

Proverbs 29:18; Isaiah 6:1-8; Acts 26:13-20.

PRAISE God for His vision.

Think of what your life would be like if God had not seen your spiritual need.

Think of what the lives of others will be like if we don't catch God's vision.

PEER into your heart.

Do you have a vision for sharing the gospel in your own community?

Do you have a vision for sharing the gospel cross-culturally?

Are you seeking to discover your place in God's plan to reach the nations?

PRAYER

Omniscient Father, I praise You for Your vision. If You hadn't seen my need, I would have no hope. Thank You for giving me an opportunity to hear about Your saving grace. Please ignite a missionary passion in my heart. I pray for people who have never heard the gospel message. Please show me how I can minister through going or supporting others who do. Help me renew my mind through reading the Bible, I want to see the world from Your perspective. I ask these things in Jesus' Name. Amen.

CHAPTER FIVE

God Gives Purpose

The morning of September 8, we left in a caravan of three canoes paddled by a dozen Sawi believers. In nine hours we traveled up the Kronkel River, south across swamp and rain forest, through a puzzle of interconnecting streams and footpaths, then down the Cook River. Some people waved as we passed, others called a greeting, but most just stared.

"See that row of huts on the south river bank?" John Mills broke into my thoughts. "Look past the huts to the shiny building near the coconut trees. The village is Kawem, and that's your house up there, Dave."

People began shouting to us. I don't know how, but the people of Kawem already had received word of our visit and were waiting to greet us. One of the first Christians I met was Waipe, who spoke Indonesian at least as well as I did. He was short and very muscular. He had a high opinion of himself and tried hard to impress me. I later learned he had a quick temper.

I met another man who walked with an awkward gait. His eyes looked dull, and I never quite grasped what he was trying to communicate. I took the word of others that he was a believer.

I heard there was a couple in Amaru who were following Jesus, but we didn't stop at Amaru during this trip. Our meeting would come later.

Haram and his wife were the third and fourth Christians I met in Kawem. Haram greeted us heartily. He was in his forties with medium height and build. His nose looked as though it had healed a little crooked after a break, but his other facial features were even and he had a pleasant smile. He spoke Indonesian well enough that he communicated his faith clearly to me. His wife, much younger, spoke only Kayagar which I couldn't understand then.

I had heard a lot about Haram; he had been the first believer among the Kayagar. Originally he had been as opposed to the gospel as others in these villages. On a hunting trip into the rain forest he became sick, to the point of death. In desperation, he sent word back to the missionary before us, John, who came into the rain forest to treat him. Impressed by such love, Haram listened to the gospel and gave his life to Christ.

In John's eyes, Haram faced a major problem. As many of the leading Kayagar men, Haram had two wives. John had advised Haram to leave one of his wives, so he had followed the missionary's counsel. Later we learned that Haram still supported his second family and visited them in secret.

Polygamy is a common custom in many tribal groups and has long caused a controversy among missionaries and national believers. In the past, most missionaries have come from Western countries where polygamy is uncommon or illegal. Biblical passages such as I Timothy 3: 2, 12 and Titus 1:6 teach that polygamy has no part in the life of a church leader. Many missionaries automatically label polygamy as sin. Some missionaries will not baptize or allow a member of a polygamous marriage to join the local church. John, the former missionary to Kawem, held this view.

I hadn't thought much about polygamy until I came head to head with the practice. As I studied Scripture and culture, I saw that polygamy is not God's ideal. He created one man and one woman and started them out together. But what if a man already has married more than one wife before he knows about God's Word? Which is the worse sin in tribal culture—polygamy or divorce? In practice, missionaries often taught that divorce is acceptable and polygamy is not. In Scripture, God never condemned polygamy, nor did He tell people to give up multiple wives. God does condemn divorce. In my thinking, if people marry according to the customs of their society, that marriage should be a lifetime bond.

Giving up all but one wife is no simple solution to polygamy. In fact, it raises many hard questions. Whom do the husbands divorce? How do they choose? Do they give up all but the first wife? Do they give up all but the youngest, strongest, or prettiest wife? Do they give up all wives except the one most likely to bear many children? What happens to the wives he does give up? How will they live? Does he have a responsibility to maintain their households? What about the children? Will they be cast out?

Kathy and I were unprepared to face such a dilemma so early in our missionary career. Should we directly disagree with what the previous missionary taught? How would this affect the people? We added this issue to our long prayer list.

John Mills and I returned to Kamur, but my attention was set on Kawem. I now had faces in my mind and issues in my heart when I prayed for the people there.

We finally moved to Kawem on November 18. We were up long before sunrise getting ready for our first flight, scheduled for six in the morning. The Mission Aviation floatplane landed right on schedule. Pilot Ed Robinson stepped from his seat to stand on the float, and called across the water, "It's moving day. Are you ready for this?"

Good question. Ed shuttled Kathy, Gwen, and me over to the Cook River where ten minutes later we landed at Kawem. While we greeted people and opened the house, Ed flew two more round trips bringing supplies.

The people of Kawem were excited to have missionaries living with them again. In our honor, they held a continuing celebration for weeks. Kathy and I tried to sleep to the deep drumbeats and a mournful sound that passed for singing. When silent, the drums were beautiful pieces of art. Each hollow drum was about three feet high and six inches around, carved with a handle. They sported various patterns depicting snakes and other animals and had a lizard-skin cover. We forgot the beauty and thought only of the inconvenience when the drums began the incessant "tum-ta-tum" and the monotonous voices began their "uuh, ohh, uuh."

In the daytime, people danced and laughed and watched our every move. We were glad the three months in Kamur had introduced us to tribal life so it didn't seem quite as strange.

Men used their time to carve elaborate designs for paddles and bows, each of which doubled as spears. They also made canoes, arrows and drums. The men hunted any bird or animal (no matter how small) to supplement their meager diet.

Before missionaries came, Kayagar men went totally nude. Then missionaries and government officials encouraged the men to wear shorts. Some continued to go nude. There didn't seem to be sexual connotations or shame associated with being naked.

The women wore only grass skirts. When a skirt started looking too ragged, they put another over it. Sometimes they wore several layers of skirts. They also made a sort of underwear of grass with a grass belt and grass hanging down in front which they pulled through their legs and hooked on the belt in back. They never took this off in public. When they went into the river, they occasionally took off the skirts, but never the "bikini" grass underwear. Even after missionaries offered dresses, most women stayed with the grass skirts. They needed easy access to nurse their children, and the grass skirts were familiar and functional. Little girls went naked until they were about five years old. Then they wore little string skirts until puberty when they graduated to grass skirts.

Women gathered sago, made food, carried water, fished, wove grass mats, and took care of children. The Kayagar used grass mats for mattresses, rugs, blankets, and carrying cases. Most mats bore a herringbone pattern. Occasionally I saw one woven in a more decorative pattern using colored grass.

Sago was the staple food. It is a starchy foodstuff derived from the soft interior of palm trees. Kathy watched the women prepare it and decided not to try that method. The women pounded it into a pulp. They made a long trough from the bark, put the pulp in it, then poured water over the pulp. This washed the flour out of the pulp and carried it down into a basin to settle. When they poured the water out of the basin, a flour was left, which they generally rolled in the two-foot long leaves of the sago palm. They overlapped the leaves and poured the flour in them, rolled the leaves tight, tied them with rattan, and put the cylinder at the edge of the fire. They seemed to know how long to leave it there, and when they took it out the crust was hard and kind of melted together. The "bread" kept several days. It was good traveling food.

From the sago, they also made something they called *papaeda*. They mixed hot water into the sago flour and it became the consistency of the old paste we used in kindergarten. Sometimes they added flavoring, but usually they just mixed it with two sticks. Then they put the sticks in their mouths and sucked the *papaeda* off them. It had no taste. Actually, kindergarten paste tastes better. The first time I ate it, someone had colored it with a red plant, and I thought I was eating congealed pig blood.

The Kayagar commonly supplemented the sago with fish, bugs, wild pigs, and birds. They ate their dogs if they got hungry, or if the dog did something they didn't like. They didn't plant crops themselves but often stole fruit the missionaries grew. If people didn't have anything else, they ate a weed that was something like spinach. I encouraged them to eat it more often because it was full of vitamin A.

The women made a ring out of rattan and wove a net onto it like a cornucopia. They carried it into the water and walked upstream hoping fish or whatever would get caught in it; this worked best during dry season when the water was low. They sometimes caught what they called "shrimp," which were more like crayfish. The women fished nearly every day since there was no refrigeration. Occasionally, they used fish line from the missionary store.

The women brought water into the house and used it without boiling or straining. The water was so full of bacteria that it turned to *uohom* (bad water) by the next day. The Kayagar had buckets by the time we arrived; but before the buckets, they used a length of bamboo about three-feet long and about three-inches thick. They stripped all the branches off but one, which they used as a handle. They pounded something inside the hollow bamboo to break off any small dividers and then filled the long hollow tube with water. A leaf held the water inside.

Being close to the river was important since it was their laundromat, bathtub, and drinking fountain all wrapped up in one not-so-neat package.

Going to the bathroom meant going to the rain forest, or maybe even through the cracks in the floor. Since the houses were on stilts, the tide came in eventually and washed everything under the houses away. With the water table that high, it was hard to build outhouses or use septic tanks or sewers.

Our house looked like a large square tin can. It was a prefabricated aluminum building, made in panels which were bolted together. The whole structure rested about three feet off the ground on ironwood posts. The missionaries before us had added a lot to the basic tin can structure, subdividing the inside into separate rooms and lining all interior walls and ceiling with woven palm bark. They had added a large outdoor kitchen for the wood stove and wired the house with a single light in each room. They had run a small electric generator for two or three hours per night to provide power. Unfortunately the generator left when they did.

We gradually unpacked and did our best to turn the house into our home. We had brought some basic furniture with us. I made bed frames and some very simple chairs, though I'm not a carpenter. Kathy sewed and put up curtains which gave us a little more privacy. We settled into a routine and began to feel more comfortable with our surroundings.

Gwen adapted quickly. She enjoyed all the attention she received. She loved to walk through the village with her friends and visit Haram's house, where she ate sago, grubs, and other local foods.

The Kayagar were happy to have us living among them because we brought many advantages. Missionary planes brought medicine, food, good tools, and other things that improved their lifestyle. The Kayagar came to us freely for physical needs, but they seemed oblivious to their spiritual needs.

When we tried to explain salvation to them, we met a wall of friendly indifference; and we didn't know how to respond. We wanted the wall to crumble, but we were unsure how to make that happen. It was frustrating, but we began to practice total reliance on God.

One of the first communication strategies I tried was using the analogy from Don Richardson's book, *Peace Child*. This had effectively illustrated the gospel message to the nearby Sawi people, and our Kayagar practiced the same custom. I explained the significance of the peace child to the Kayagar, "Look at this example in your own culture. Don't you see how this points to Jesus Christ?"

They looked at me and said, in effect, "So what?"

When that didn't work, I tried introducing them to John 3:16 which I had often used when telling people about Christ. "For God so loved the world that he gave his only begotten Son..."

One man responded by asking, "What is love?" The Kayagar had no word that meant love as God loved. In my unfamiliarity with the culture, I could not transfer this concept from my mind to theirs. Frustration increased. They were still in darkness, and I didn't know how to enlighten them. They were dying without Christ, and I didn't know how to lead them to eternal life.

Eternity was another concept they didn't understand. I found I couldn't talk to them about eternal life because they lived day to day. Haupm, an older Kayagar man, gently chided me, "Dafid, if I have enough food for today and tomorrow, why would I even think about the days after that? This eternity you talk about is strange to our ears."

Kathy and I felt confused by the response to our message; we didn't know what to do. We had always known God had to do the real work in a person's heart, but now this became more real to us. We could explain something clearly to a physically dead man, but he couldn't hear, understand, or believe it. Only God could give him life and understanding. We were realizing more and more that no matter how much of the language we learned, how much of Kayagar culture we understood, or how clearly we explained spiritual truths to spiritually dead people, they could not understand or believe them. Only God could give spiritual understanding and life.

While waiting for God to reveal His plan, we fell into a routine of secondary ministries. We opened a station store called a *toko*. Every mission station in Irian Jaya seemed to have one, so we did too. We sold new items like soap, fishhooks, salt, and clothing. Though this wasn't our main reason for coming to Irian Jaya, we were providing a helpful service. There wasn't enough market to entice a "real" store in that area.

We didn't receive relief shipments. Every time we went to the coast for vacation, we set aside one full day to shop for the *toko*. We tried to get the lowest prices for our people and sold everything for our cost. We packed things up and brought them to the MAF base in Sentani. MAF flew them to Kawem for their operating costs.

People were earning money by working for the school system, the government, or us. If cash salaries were to mean anything to them, they had to have something to purchase with that cash. The local government set costs and salaries for each area. Many times we wanted to pay more, but the government didn't allow that freedom.

We also opened a medical clinic, where I did most of the work. Handing out aspirin and vitamins did more good than harm, and giving penicillin shots often helped fight tropical infections. I also learned more about the Kayagar culture as I interacted with them in the clinic. For example, most people thought the magic of an injection was in the point, not the medicine inside. They reasoned that the needle made a little hole in the skin so sickness could escape from the body. I delivered babies, sewed up arrow wounds, and did some minor surgery. I even saved lives. When I couldn't handle a situation, I could get advice from a missionary doctor over our two-way radio. In emergencies, we could even airlift patients to a hospital operated by The Evangelical Alliance Mission (TEAM). Kathy and I did what we could with what we had, because we cared about the Kayagar people's physical needs.

I "charged" the people a low fee (some sago or whatever). We didn't want to create dependence, and we wanted the people to value the medicine. If I hadn't charged, giving stuff away would have consumed all my time. Giving things only to believers would have encouraged people to claim belief just to get something. So we tried our best to help the people in every way.

Still, we had a great burden. We hadn't traveled halfway around the world just to poke holes in people's skin. We weren't there just to disperse vitamins or sell salt. We were there to introduce the Kayagar to Jesus Christ, and we didn't know how to do this.

While we prayed for a miracle to open Kayagar hearts, God was doing a spiritual work in our own lives. When we came to a place where we lacked confidence in ourselves and human understanding, when we felt confused and realized we lacked the necessary knowledge and wisdom to do this work, we returned to complete reliance on God and began to develop patience.

Only then did the Lord show us our purpose is to glorify Him in everything we do, and trust Him to use it however He wills. He was preparing the scene for something special, even if we weren't aware of it.

CHAPTER FIVE APPLICATION GUIDE

"And whatsoever ye do in word or deed, do all in the name of the Lord Jesus, giving thanks to God and the Father by him" Colossians 3:17.

We were made to reflect glory back to our Creator. (Isaiah 43:7) We can dedicate even the smallest word or action to God's glory. Parents can pray for their children while changing diapers, folding clothes, and washing dishes. Employees can work as unto their Lord and Master. Children can obey their parents, do homework, and pick up toys because they love God. Fathers can disciple their children through daily examples. For God's glory, consider some of these actions:

Encourage one another with kind words.

Smile or give a cup of cold water in Christ's name. (Mark 9:41)
Visit shut-ins, nursing homes, and jails.
Serve as a big brother to the fatherless.
Read a book to a child or blind person.

Our life is made up of common small thoughts, words, and actions. No thought is unimportant. No word is unimportant. No action is unimportant. God sees our motives (purpose) for each one and blesses us according to His plan.

Though Dave and Kathy had learned many lessons before they arrived in Irian Jaya, God was still teaching them more. Three important lessons they learned were:

1) Adapting to God's time schedule brings the best results.
2) Building close relationships is necessary for effective ministry.
3) Celebrating God in whatever we do brings Him glory.

PONDER these Scriptures:

Matthew 5:16; Romans 12:1-2; I Peter 2:11-12.

PRAISE God for designing us to glorify Him.

Name some ways others have blessed you and glorified God.

Name three things you can do to bless others and glorify God.

PEER into your heart.

Are you willing to perform mundane tasks with proper motives?

Will you do everything you do for the glory of God? (Colossians 3:17)

PRAYER

Father, I praise You because You give good gifts to Your children. Thank You for giving me purpose in all I do. I pray that everything I think, say, and do will glorify You. Please help me remember this as I go about my daily life. Please forgive me when my motives are selfish and help me repent. Please help me encourage others as they serve You. I pray in the Name of Your Son, Jesus, may others see my works and glorify my Father in heaven. Amen.

Photos

Dave & Kathy Tucker

As the Tuckers prepared to leave for Irian Jaya in April of 1975, they gathered with family for a last informal family snapshot in the parking lot of Hawthorne Gospel Church. (l. to r.) Dave's parents Bob Tucker and Doris Tucker, Dave, Kathy, Dot Hazen, Barb Hazen, Debbie Hazen, Bob Hazen, Gwen, Barney Hazen.

Kathy and Dave Tucker were commissioned at Hawthorne Gospel Church prior to being sent to Irian Jaya. Standing, second to right is Joseph F. Conley, U.S. Director of the Regions Beyond Missionary Union. To the far right is Pastor Herrmann G. Braunlin, founding pastor of Hawthorne Gospel Church.

Dave asked the men of Amaru to “dress up” and reenact some of their stories of the old days. These men were showing Dave how they would raid another village.

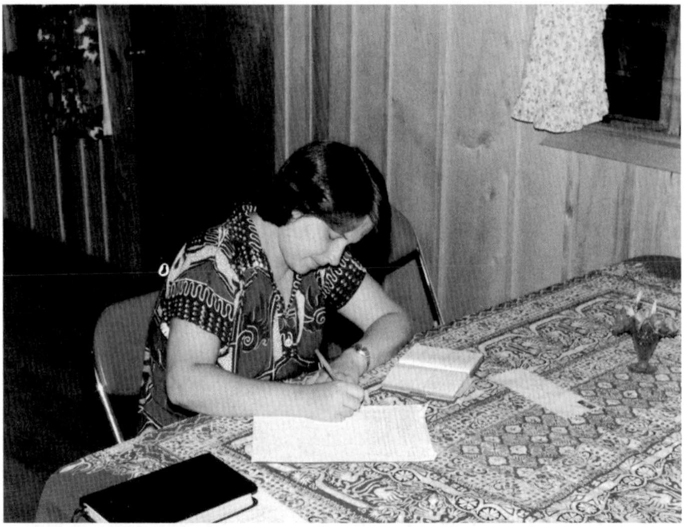

Kathy's diaries helped reconstruct many of the stories in this book. Here Kathy is using the diary to write a letter home in the early 1980s.

A Tucker family photo taken at Karubaga in 1978. (l. to r.) Gwen, Kathy, Dave, Kristen. We were in Karubaga for the annual RBMU Field Conference. Graham Cousens took this shot for us.

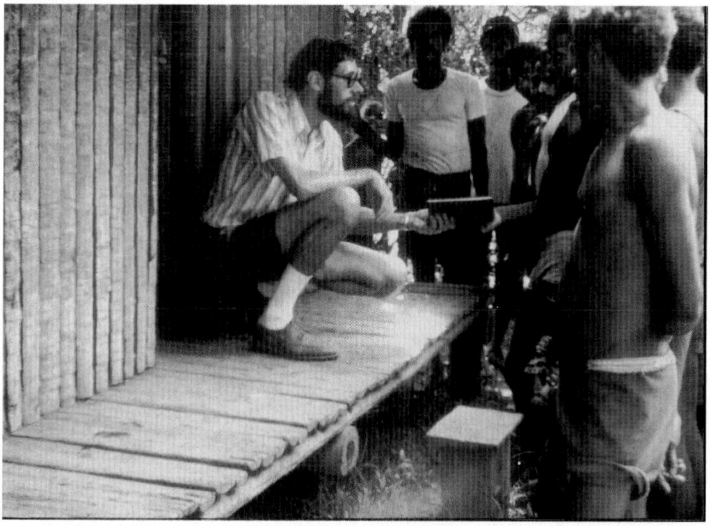

The pivotal event in this book was the day the people of Kaipom village came to Kawem to talk to Dave. The events of that day helped bring this entire village to faith in Christ and opened the door to the church planted on the Cook River.

Kayagar elders Tadeus (second from right) and Haram (far right) baptizing two men in the Cook River next to Kawem village.

The first observance of the Lord's Supper among the newly formed Klassis Kokor. Held at Kawem village.

Dave woke early one morning and went outside with his new camera to catch the sunrise. Instead he found this group of girls standing in the village mist.

Dave's present position in SEND International gives the opportunity to travel and minister around the world. Here he is at the Pelnig Baptist Church near Sofia, Bulgaria. Dave has just preached two sermons in the house church and is sitting between the pastor and his wife.

A photo of Kawem village looking peaceful and somewhat beautiful in high water. During flood season, the water would rise to floor level on these houses. During the dry season all of this ground was bone dry.

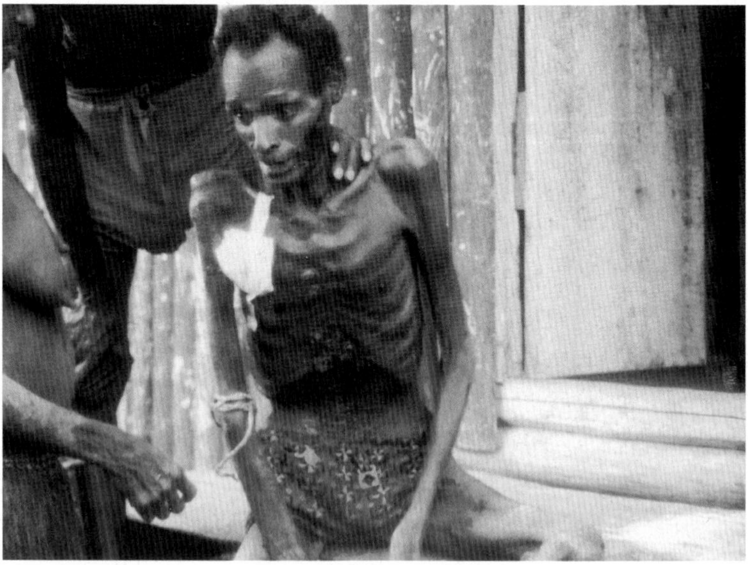

Sickness was a fact of life for the Kayagar as well as the missionaries. If they lived outside of the immediate Kawem area, people would often wait to bring patients to Dave until it was too late. Many times those who thought they were dying would just stop eating, which most often turned into a self-fulfilling prophecy.

CHAPTER SIX

God Gives Joy

"Something's wrong!" I shouted when Kathy and I woke up December 24. The silence was unnerving. For the first time since we moved to Kawem the drums were quiet.

"Where is everyone?" Kathy asked as we looked from our window to the empty village. "There are always children running around our yard at this time of morning and adults lining up for clinic. I can't even see any dogs, chickens, or pigs."

"Kak, wait 'til you hear this." I rushed back into the house after walking through the village. "Almost everyone is in the rain forest gathering food for Christmas Day. Is their only understanding of Christianity feasting?"

"You know, Dave, many people in our culture only think of Christmas as feasting and gifts, too. Maybe we can show the Kayagar the true meaning."

"I have to admit, my thoughts about them being gone weren't that spiritual either."

"What do you mean?" Kathy asked.

"Well, first I wondered how they could go off without telling me. Then I thought about how quiet it is and how much office work I could do this morning."

I'm sure my tasks seemed important at the time; now I can't even remember what I was doing when God called me to His work. Hearing a commotion out on the river about ten yards from our house, I walked from my office and saw a river covered with canoes filled with people, and they were headed straight at me.

Made from hollowed-out tree trunks, the average canoe was about fifteen-feet long and eighteen-inches wide. The people stood up to paddle, so the paddles were extra long. Since it was difficult to carry a weapon while they paddled, they designed their paddles for double duty. The beautifully carved bottoms moved the canoes along smoothly. Tipped by the toenail of a cassowary bird, these paddles also served as deadly spears. The cassowary is a flightless bird just shorter than an ostrich, and it can disembowel a man with one kick.

Canoes overturn easily, so the people devised a special way of disembarking. They brought the canoe to shore quickly. When it hit the mud, the front went up and the first person hopped off (which lightened the canoe). Then it went farther, and the next person hopped off. Though it is fascinating to watch this, I had other things on my mind that day.

Soon a large crowd of people holding dangerous looking paddles surrounded me and stared at me with no facial expression. I was a bit nervous, to say the least. "Hi, guys. What are you doing here?" I tried to sound nonchalant.

"We came for medicine."

Relief flooded over me. *Medicine. I can handle that quickly and they'll be on their way soon.*

I walked them to the clinic building trying to think positively. *They'll tell me what's wrong, I'll give them medicine, they'll go down the steps...*

The first man broke into my reverie as he stepped up to my window.

"*Bekem hamohom?*" I asked ("What is your sickness?")

"*Fo,*" (cough) and he coughed to prove it. I gave him some cough medicine. He grimaced when he swallowed, but then he seemed happy.

"*Bekem hamohom?*" I repeated to the second man.

"*Fo,*" was the reply again

Several people trailed across with "*fo.*" Then it changed, and the next ten or so people had another complaint (all the same). We went through the entire village of Kaipom with about four main complaints. Everyone looked remarkably healthy and happy once they got their medicine. *"What is happening?"* I thought.

When I had treated everyone in line, I looked out the window. "Anyone else?"

"No," the spokesman said.

"Can I close the clinic?"

"Yes, close up."

I left the clinic and walked over to them. "What do you want to do now?"

"We're going home." I waited, but they made no move to leave.

"Do you want to talk to me?"

"No, we're going home."

"Can I go back to my office?"

"Yes, you go back to work. We'll just go home to our village."

With a sense of relief I walked back to my office. *The excitement's over; I can get back to work now.*

As I picked up my pen, I had a weird feeling—as if every eye in the world was focused at the back of my head. Looking out the window, I saw dozens of eyes peering over the windowsill at me. I walked to the office door and looked out. "Can I do anything for you?"

"No."

"What are you doing?"

"Watching you."

Oh wonderful, I thought. "Are you sure you don't want to talk to me?"

"No, you can go back in your office."

I tried to get back to work, but there were the eyes again, boring into the back of my head. I prayed, "Lord, please help me understand what's going on."

He impressed me with the thought that I wasn't going to get any work done anyway, so I might as well stay outside with them. Again I went out. "Look, there is nothing important I have to do today. Why don't I just sit here and talk with you a while?"

For the first time that day I began to see some smiles. I could almost hear them thinking, *This man has finally figured out that we want to talk to him.*

I sat down on the porch of the office and started talking to these men about everyday things. We discussed how many canoes people owned and pigs that ran around the village, just general conversation in Irian Jaya. I was surprised how much I enjoyed being with them.

I learned some of the men's names; they already knew to call me by my first name, which they pronounced as Dafit. Many Indonesians give missionaries the honorific title *Tuan*. I felt that put an unnecessary distance between us, so I discouraged this. Sometimes they called me *bapak*, a term that showed respect and means something like the English mister. I enjoyed the respect, but felt I could more easily minister to them as Dafit.

The people who lived in the village of Kaipom were from the Autohoim tribe. I already knew they were a small tribe, divided among just three villages. They survived by attaching themselves to other nearby tribes. Kaipom identified themselves with the Kayagar tribe, so they knew the language I was learning. Though they also had their own tribal language, many of them spoke Indonesian well enough to chat with me.

Kornelius seemed to speak Indonesian best and fell naturally into the role of village spokesman.

As we were talking, I noticed two men being pushed forward from the back of the crowd. When they were standing right under my nose, Kornelius said, "Dafit, do you see these two men?"

"Yes, I can see them, Kornelius."

"These men have stopped smoking, and they want to read."

I just stared between Kornelius and the two men. *What in the world is that supposed to mean?* Fortunately I didn't say this out loud.

I sat, stunned, until the Lord supplied spiritual insight. He helped me hear not just the words these people were saying, but what they were thinking. "Stopped smoking?" I knew they had noticed that the missionaries didn't smoke. *They must think if they stop smoking, they'll be Christians.*

"They want to read." *What are Christian missionaries doing all the time? Reading! We read the Bible, work on Bible translation, and teach converts to read. Even when we're not working, we always seem to be reading something.* (What else can one do in the rain forest?) *They must be reasoning that since Christians read, they'll be Christians if they learn to read.*

I know that smoking and reading do not determine salvation. At another time I might have wanted to argue that as a point of theology. But that day I was attuned enough that I could understand what they were trying to say.

God also gave me wisdom about what to do next. Without a word in reply I moved back into the office and took two copies of Luke's Gospel in very simple Indonesian. When I placed these books in the hands of those two men, they were delighted. They looked at the books and held them up so everybody could see. They couldn't read the books; but they had communicated a need, and I had responded in a way that pleased them.

I wasn't quite sure what was happening. A friend of mine has since said that I was unconsciously competent. I didn't know why I was doing some of what I was; but since God was guiding, I did the right things. On that day I only knew something special was happening, so I tried to keep the momentum going. "You have done a good thing here today. There is much more that I want to say to you. But I know you want to go to your village soon. You don't want to be on the river at night. We don't have time to talk more now, but can I come to your village next week and spend more time with you?"

Big smiles came to their faces as they burst into excited chatter. "Good, Dafit," was all they said to me, but I knew I had said the right thing.

They wanted me to come immediately, but I couldn't do that. Now I had to find a way to schedule that visit. Talking about a day of the week or time would not help them because they didn't have watches, calendars, or even a concept of scheduled time. Remembering something another missionary had told me, I found a piece of string and tied seven knots in it. I gave it to their leader and said, "Every time the sun comes up, cut one knot off this string. When there are no more knots on the string, come back and I'll go with you to your village."

Kathy came out of the house about this time and stood by me. Immediately, two older women came out of the crowd. One of these ladies took me by the arm and led me away from the others. She tried to explain what she was doing, but I didn't understand her. With no idea of what was going on, I glanced over my shoulder and noticed the second woman taking Kathy in the opposite direction.

My new friend took a lump of sago, their staple food, rubbed it on my arm and popped it into her mouth. I looked at my arm and then at her, while she smiled at me toothlessly. Knowing that these people were cannibals not so long ago, I quickly returned to the security of the group and worked my way to Kornelius.

"What did this woman do to me?" I asked.

"Dafit, you responded to what we did and said. This woman has adopted you into her family. She wanted to show you much she appreciates what you've done for us and what you are going to do for us. The other woman did the same thing to your wife. Your family is now part of our village."

To this day, Kathy and I are related to virtually everybody in Kaipom.

With that, the people of Kaipom piled into their canoes and set off down the river. Everything had happened so quickly, Kathy and I stood there with our heads spinning. As we watched the canoes disappear around a bend in the Cook River, we wondered what would come from this day. All we could do was wait.

We gave our concerns to the Lord and focused on celebrating Christ's birth. Christmas morning we opened presents, listened to the radio, and walked through the village. We had a church service at noon and ate a chicken dinner. It was a much different Christmas from our past holidays, but it was a pleasant time. Stripped of commercialism, Christmas in the rain forest allowed us to reflect on its true meaning. The angel's voice of Luke 2:10 took on a new meaning and foreshadowed our ministry to the Kayagar: "...Behold, I bring you good tidings of great joy, which shall be to all people."

The next morning we experienced an earthquake, and then it was time for the clinic, and then we had visitors... And so the week passed all too quickly.

I heard the river come alive with canoes again. There were possibly even more people than before, but at least I knew who they were and why they were coming. The paddles didn't look quite as threatening this week.

It was about two hours by canoe to Kaipom. These canoes were not built for sitting. To fit my hips into it, I had to turn sideways and twist myself in until I was stuck. When I tried standing and balancing in the shaky canoe, one of my hosts asked ominously, "Dafit, do you know how to swim?" So I sat, wedged in tightly as we rocked down the river.

It seems that the Autohoim figured that missionaries were always looking for new airstrip sites, since this was our primary means of transportation and supply. Most villages wanted an airstrip because of the money and prestige it offered. So the first stop on my village tour was what they considered prime airstrip land. I really wasn't airstrip hunting that day and was honestly disappointed that this seemed to be their primary concern. I was trying to tell them tactfully it wouldn't work since it was under about nine inches of water.

"Well," I said kicking at a little clump of dirt, "this place is flat and level, but it would take a bit of work."

They laughed, and it suddenly occurred to me that they were not serious about it. They were going through the motions because they thought I expected it.

The tour continued through the village. Since I was a newly adopted member of their family, they explained each house. "So-and-so built this house. His family lives there and these are all the people in his family." Mothers held their babies out the window so I could meet them. I love children, so I would take them in my arms, throw them up in the air and catch them. The kids screamed, the mothers screamed, but everyone enjoyed the attention.

My new family walked me through the village, and then they took me to the "men's house." This long structure was the center of power in any village. Only initiated adult males were allowed to enter the building.

While the men took me into the single room, the women and older children gathered around the outside walls to peer through cracks and listen to what was going on. As we crowded in I thought, *Oh boy, this is a full day of new missionary experiences.*

"Dafit, would you like to eat some of this?" It was lunchtime, and they had been preparing for me. Now Kornelius squatted next to me with a plate full of food in his hand.

"Do you eat it?" I had learned not to ask what I was eating—most times I didn't really want to know. But this question was important. Once when I had asked this question, my host replied, "Oh no, we can't eat this; it might kill our people."

That day all the food was safe. I must have had the missionary equivalent of a sixteen-course banquet that day—a little bit of everything.

When Kornelius asked, "How about something to drink?" I shuddered at the thought. All I could picture was the local river water. A small organism in the water turned it a reddish-brown color. I knew the several villages upstream used the water as a floating garbage disposal, and I didn't even want to think about what was in that river.

Trying hard not to gag, I said, "What do you have for me to drink?"

"We'll make some tea." Breathing a sigh of relief, I knew I could handle that. Tea leaves would color the water and I wouldn't notice how dirty it was. Boiling would purify it.

As it turned out, they must have taken a couple of tea leaves, dropped them in a big pot, and waved it over a fire from a safe distance. They brought me a pot of lukewarm river water with a little extra color. I prayed silently, "Lord, You brought me here for a purpose, and I hope it doesn't include death by tea. I will trust your protection right now." I drank the tea.

I had noticed throughout the meal that none of the men had eaten anything with me. I began to realize they were testing me. Accepting their hospitality proved to them I cared about them. The Lord was working in me as well as in them. At some level I was aware that I was connecting with these men and women in a way I normally would not have been able to do. God had given me love and joy to share with these people.

When they cleared away all the food, every man in the village came into the room and sat facing me. The women were still outside the house, watching and listening. Kornelius found his way to my side again and said, "Dafit, tell us why you're here."

My mind reeled. Not knowing what to expect from that day, I hadn't come with a prepared agenda. Again, I needed the Lord's wisdom. *Where should I begin? How could I effectively explain the gospel to people who had never heard it before?* I had years' worth of important information to say in a few minutes. I realized with a shock I had only as long as I could hold their attention to tell them everything they needed to know to make a conscious decision to follow Christ. With a quick prayer and a deep breath I began talking.

I started with the first chapter and verse of Genesis and moved quickly through creation, the fall of mankind, and the call of Abraham. I tried to establish God's right over His creation and His provision for salvation, especially noting the connection through Abraham's line. Then I took a quick jump to Matthew and explained how God did something about the fall—Jesus Christ. I dashed though His life and death, demonstrating His right to be our means of salvation. I told them about the resurrection and that Jesus Christ is a living God.

As I came to the end, about thirty minutes later, I faced the question of how to explain salvation. In our Western culture we often use phrases such as "be converted" or "get saved" or "accept Christ" or "ask Jesus into your heart." These terms rarely make sense to people outside North America, let alone tribal people with no Christian background. I had put a good deal of prayer and thought into my terminology, and I thought I had found words they could understand.

I had studied how tribal people follow their leaders, the village chief or head of their clan. Tribal people follow a leader by giving allegiance to that person, by doing what he says, and by accepting the leader's judgment and decisions—basically committing themselves to that person. In their culture, "follow" seemed to sum up true faith in Christ; and I had decided to use that terminology.

Knowing how tribal people make decisions was as important as using the right words. Like most people from my American culture, I was used to making decisions on my own. Individualism is a virtue in our country. Tribal people, though, make decisions as a group. They often talk through issues and spend days, weeks, or even months in discussion before coming to a decision. When the group makes a decision, everyone follows. This is not just a vote; it is decision by consensus—true unanimity.

That could be just a very interesting insight at almost any other time. But now it was crucial. As I was trying to tell them the basics of Christianity, it had a tremendous bearing on how I would finish. I could not just call for a show of hands or encourage individuals to follow Christ. If I did not persuade the entire group to transfer their allegiance to Christ, I would probably lose them all.

These thoughts lay heavy in my mind as I finished my discourse, and I was not sure where to go next. After a moment of silence, I told them, "Look, no matter what happens here—whether you say yes or no to God—I will be your friend. You can come to me for medicine when you're sick and supplies when you need them. You can visit and talk with me almost any time. I will be your friend. But if you say yes to God, you will have a much better friend. God is a friend who will never leave you."

At that point I stopped. I had said everything I could. It was up to them to make some sort of decision. They immediately began talking among themselves in their own language. Their faces were expressionless; I had no idea what they were saying. I sat watching them, alternately praying that they would follow Christ and wondering what I would do if they rejected salvation. My thoughts flew. *This isn't even the tribal group I am supposed to work with. This isn't even the language I'm learning. Lord, this is Your work; please do something!*

After about twenty minutes of them talking and me waiting, I saw heads nodding. They were reaching a decision. Kornelius was again the spokesman. He turned to me and said, "*Bapak, kami mau ikut Tuhan Yesus.*" (Sir, we do want to follow Jesus Christ.)

Relief and joy overwhelmed me! This was why I was here. In the midst of my excitement, though, I began to wonder, *Do they really understand?* Asking for permission to talk again, I repeated nearly everything I had told them earlier. They listened politely; then said, "Dafit, we really did understand it the first time, but it's good to hear it again so soon."

It was real. God had opened their spiritual eyes and ears. Joy filled them.

I have to admit that I didn't fully understand what happened on that day. Over the next five years we were able to put together the whole story. From the time Kathy and I arrived in Kawem these people of Kaipom had been attracted to our faith. They heard what we preached and agreed among themselves that it seemed good.

"We can live with this belief," they agreed at a village gathering.

"But how can we be sure that it is true? We don't know this woman and man. How can we know that they are speaking honestly? Do they want something from us? Are they trying to use us as so many have done before? How can we know?"

As a group, they decided to test us. "You go and ask for medicine," the chief pointed to one man. "Tell us how he treats you. Will he accept you as an equal, or just a body to examine?"

"You, children and young men, go stand in their yard and stare at them. See if the man or woman come out and talk to you."

We must have passed the tests. As a group, they decided we were trustworthy. In their minds, then, they could trust our words and our teaching. Now they wanted to hear the message firsthand. When they all arrived in our yard on that Christmas Eve, their intention was to get us to come visit their village. It is amazing the way God worked out all the details.

By the time I visited Kaipom, they were ready to accept my words—actually God's word—and do whatever I asked them to do. When they understood what I said and the invitation I offered that day in the men's house, they were primed and ready to follow Jesus. They made that decision in a culturally relevant way and so made Christ their own.

Over the next years, things began to add up. While Kathy and I had been praying for God's guidance and feeling confused, He was already busy preparing Autohoim hearts. Even though we were frustrated about just doing "secondary ministry," He was using these acts of kindness to set everything up for this day. God truly is loving, sufficient, wise, generous, and joyful.

CHAPTER SIX APPLICATION GUIDE

"When you obey Me you are living in My love, just as I obey My Father and live in His love. I have told you this so that you will be filled with My joy. Yes, your cup of joy will overflow!" John 15:10-11 (TLNT).

The preceding verses tell us we must live in Christ and let Him live in us to produce the fruit of the Holy Spirit. He uses the example of a branch severed from the vine trying to produce fruit on its own. Sounds ridiculous, doesn't it? Yet we sometimes think we can neglect our relationship with God and still produce the fruit of God's Holy Spirit.

Joy comes not from where you are but what you are. Dave and Kathy left many comforts, faithfully obeying God under difficult circumstances; He filled their hearts with joy. Dave shared

God's Word with the Kaipom people and they turned from their sin to follow God; He filled their hearts with joy. When people respond to God and obey Him, all heaven rejoices.

Sometimes Christians go through hard times. Is joy possible even then? I believe it is when we trust God fully and keep our eyes on the end result of our faith. Jesus did this. (See Hebrews 12:1-2).

God has an inexhaustible well of joy we can drink from and quench our thirst. We can even be saturated until we cannot contain all the joy and it overflows to others. If this is not happening in our lives, what should we do?

Francis of Assisi said, "If you, O servant of God, are upset, for any reason whatever, you should immediately rise up to prayer, and you should remain in the presence of the Most High Father for as long as it takes for Him to restore to you the joy of your salvation."

PONDER these Scriptures:

Psalm 51:10-12; I Thessalonians 1:6; I Peter 1:3-9.

PRAISE God for joy which doesn't depend on our surroundings.

Think about a time you felt joy bubbling up from deep within you.

Have you ever felt joy or observed others feeling joy during difficult times?

PEER into your heart.

Are you full of joy?

If not, what will you do about it?

PRAYER

Joyful Jesus, Thanks for enduring the cross, while focusing on the joy You would attain. Through Your example I know joy can be mine no matter the circumstances. Please help me keep a vital, intimate relationship with our heavenly Father. Please help me display the joy that comes only from the Holy Spirit. Thank You that no one can take Your joy from me. I pray for those who depend on the world for happiness and never feel deep joy. Please fill Your servants around the world with Your joy, and through their lives draw people from every tongue and every nation into a blissful relationship with You. Amen.

CHAPTER SEVEN

God Gives Faith

While I still sat in the Kaipom men's house, I talked to the men about their need for discipleship. "Now that you are following Tuhan Yesus, I want to help you learn God's ways."

"Yes," they chorused. "Move here so you and your wife can teach us every day."

"No, I can't move here. My mission agency told me to live in Kawem and teach all the Kayagar about Jesus. If I live here, I will be too far away to help other villages like Amiyam."

There was a moment of disappointed silence, then Kornelius spoke up again. "We do understand that, Dafit. Now that we are following Tuhan Yesus, we know how important it is for other villages to do the same thing. You're right. You have to help them. But who will help us?"

"We are all like little babies." An older man named Au spoke up, pointing at my Bible. "The words you have in that book are like food to make us grow strong. But we can't read those words. How will we know what God expects of us? We need a teacher."

His spiritual insight startled me. Now was the time for me to go out on a limb. "There are some villages far from here where the people have been following Jesus for a long time. Would you like me to ask one of those men to live in Kaipom and teach you God's ways?"

I saw heads nodding assents, so I made an additional offer. "Many other villages have government schools to teach the children how to read and write. Since the government has not started a school here in Kaipom, would you like me to find a schoolteacher for you?"

They broke into excited smiles, then asked, "Why would you do all of this for us?"

"Last week you adopted Kathy and I into this village. Today God adopted you into His family. Why are you surprised that I would help my new fathers, mothers, sisters, and brothers?"

There are no short conversations in a tribal culture, and this one was no exception. Over the next hour or so I repeated my commitments to provide an evangelist to teach them God's Word and a teacher to establish a Christian grade school for their children. They promised, in turn, to provide the evangelist and teacher with food, firewood, and other necessities. They also assured me they would construct a school, church building, and houses for the evangelist and teacher.

When I got home, I burst in the door and grabbed Kathy. I told her the news as I swung her around the kitchen in my arms. The girls watched and laughed at our excitement.

After supper, Kathy settled into a chair next to our oil lamp and opened the mailbag that had arrived earlier in the day. "Listen to this, Dave," Kathy said. "The Johnsons had triplets! Elinor writes, 'even though they knew about it in advance, the reality of caring for three new babies overwhelmed them.' She gives some more details, and then says, 'The church put out a call for help, and the ladies organized a work schedule so Mrs. Johnson would always have someone around to help her.'"

I didn't know the Johnsons well, so I didn't pay too much attention until Kathy added, "This is where we are, isn't it? We're overwhelmed with the care of a whole village full of new babes in Christ. Since we can't call on a local church full of volunteers, what will we do?"

"I'm not sure, Kak, but they're His new babies, and He won't neglect them."

The next day I made a radio call to John Dekker, the RBMU missionary working with the Dani church leadership. The Dani tribe, living in the western highlands of Irian Jaya, had responded to the gospel in a series of tremendous people movements. This happened in the late 1950s and early 1960s. Since then, their churches had developed their own missionary vision. By the time we were settled in Kawem, Dani churches from the Toli Valley area supported hundreds of their own missionaries. Maybe they could provide the help we needed. "John, something tremendous has happened here. I'll tell you details some other time, but right now I need some help from the church up there. Can you find an evangelist and a grade school teacher?"

All this was new to me, but John had been there before. "No problem," came John's distinctive Dutch accent. I smiled at Kathy across the radio when we heard this. This was John's normal response to any opportunity. "I can't promise anything before I talk to the church leaders, but I suspect we will have good news. I'll get back to you in a day or so."

It took only that long before God enabled John and the Dani church to come through for us. John radioed back on January 12 that he had found us a teacher and an evangelist.

When the floatplane came into Kawem a few weeks later, I met our new teacher, Naftali Tebai. Looking behind him, I was surprised to see Mbitmber and his family in the plane. Mbitmber had been living in Amiyam just before we first arrived on the south coast. He had been with John Mills and me when we went to Kawam by canoe. Then he had gone home to his Dani village of Kanggime for a scheduled rest. Because he had departed so soon after we arrived, I hadn't had time to get to know him well. Later, I learned he had graduated from the *Sekolah Alkitab Maranata* (Maranatha Bible School) in Karubaga and had years of experience in ministry. Mbitmber and his brother, Timotius, had worked as evangelists to the Kayagar before Kathy and I came. Mbitmber and his family had lived in Amiyam and ministered faithfully.

Mbitmber was in Kanggime when the Kaipom movement began, so he first heard the news when John began looking for my helpers. Now he listened as I described the Kaipom situation to Tebai. When I finished, he whispered, as if to himself, "This is why God spared my life and brought me here." In a louder voice he announced, "My family and I are going to Kaipom."

Seeing my stunned look, he explained how he had reached this decision. "Dafit, before you came here I had an accident in a canoe. I fell into the river and hit my head on a log. I was under water for a long time. When the people pulled me from the river they were sure I was dead. But God raised me up. When I realized that He had given me more years of life, I promised Him I would spend those years serving Him in this area. When I heard about what God had done in Kaipom, God touched my heart again. I knew He had spared me so I could work in this village. I talked this over with my wife and my children, and we all agree Kaipom will be our next home."

What could I say? Kathy and I could only praise God for once again moving ahead of us. He had an overall plan for this area and was bringing so many pieces together in this plan that only He could keep track of them all. We were two of those pieces. We had just met two more.

By the end of February, Tebai and Mbitmber settled into their new homes in Kaipom. The villagers had upheld their part of the bargain. Waiting for them were two new houses, stocked with food and firewood. Behind the houses was something this village had never seen before—a three-room schoolhouse. All three buildings stood on stilts with the floors about three feet above the ground. The frames were round poles tied together with vines, the floors long slices of palm bark laid over the poles, the walls of *gaba-gaba* cut from the sago palm tree. A fresh smell permeated the buildings from the newly cut sago leaves which formed the roofs. The walls of the school building didn't go all the way to the roof, leaving a foot-wide gap for light and ventilation. This primitive construction made three of the most beautiful buildings I had ever seen.

Finding and placing the teachers was only one of the challenges we faced in establishing our school in Kaipom. Ordering and receiving books, pencils, and writing paper from the capital would take time. In the meantime, I had to provide teaching materials and advise Tebai, and I was no expert on grade schools in Irian Jaya. I arranged for a portrait of Suharto, Indonesia's president, to hang in each classroom and bought charts, maps, and flags. Then I made chalkboards out of plywood and a special blackboard paint.

When my blackboards were ready in mid-March, I decided to deliver them in person. Loading everything into our motorboat, I arrived down river in Kaipom at about ten o'clock in the morning. I decided to make the visit a surprise, so I turned off the motor before everyone could hear it and drifted the last few hundred yards to the riverbank near the school.

No one had seen me. I saw some women fishing downriver, but they didn't notice me. Singing came from one classroom and the sound of Tebai teaching from another. I quietly followed the sound of Tebai's voice until I suddenly appeared in the door of his classroom. He and his students were surprised. I was shocked beyond words!

"*Selamat pagi, Bapak* Dafit," they chorused when they noticed me in the doorway.

Not to return their "Good morning," was rude, but I really couldn't speak. I had expected to see the benches filled with Autohoim boys and girls, and I did. But there, sitting among the six, seven, eight-year-old children were the twenty to thirty-year-old men of the village. In Kayagar and Autohoim culture, it was unthinkable to see adults and children sitting together in a formal setting like church or school. In fact, it was considered humiliating for an adult to sit with children.

Seeing the bewildered look on my face, twenty-year-old Esime stood up. "Dafit, are you surprised to see us like this? You know us well enough to understand we men don't do this, but we want to read. You and Mbitmber told us it's important to know God's Word. Right now you're here to tell us what God's Word says, but we men decided we have to learn to read it for ourselves so we can follow God's ways. We agreed that we're willing to humble ourselves and learn with the children because God's Word is so important."

"You're doing a very good thing," was all I could say. Truly, God was working here, molding the lives of these people into His image. He was changing their deepest thought processes.

Finally, I remembered my cultural manners and greeted everyone, "*Selamat pagi.*"

"Dafit," Esime grinned, "we are learning to read in Indonesian." He held up a children's book. "I can almost read this book already. Soon I'll be able to read this." He lifted the Gospel of Luke I had placed in his hands three months earlier.

The people in other villages along the Cook and Kronkel Rivers turned their attention on these special happenings in Kaipom, and this provided many witnessing opportunities. Later that same week one of the older men of Kawem came alongside me as I walked through the village.

"Dafit, we've noticed that you are spending a lot of time in Kaipom."

This statement is more than a casual observation. Maybe I'll have a chance to witness to him. "That's right, Han. The people of Kaipom have decided to follow Jesus. Now I'm helping them learn God's Word."

"I'm so happy to hear that," Han replied. "I'm a Christian, too."

I stopped and looked into his eyes. Many people called themselves Christian if they lived in a village with a Protestant missionary, or if they just sat in the church. *Is this what Han thought?*

"Han, I know you come to church, but there's more to being a Christian than that."

"I know that, Dafit. I believe in Jesus and have been following Him just like you and the people of Kaipom. He saved me from my sins."

Seeing the stunned look on my face, Han answered my unasked question. "No, I never told you about it. I didn't know how you would react. You see, the missionary who used to live here was *kakup*—very strong and set in his way. When some of our people in Kawem became Christians, he heaped burdens on their heads. Then he was very upset if we did not live up to those burdens. It seemed to us that he wanted us to be just like him, but we couldn't do that. We are Kayagar, not like your people. We were afraid to tell him we were Christians.

"When you and your wife came here, we thought you would be *kakup* like the other man, so we didn't tell you we were real Christians. Now we see how you are treating the new Christians in Kaipom. You are not giving them heavy burdens. Instead you are helping them learn slowly. You are being patient and helping them to grow.

"We like you and the way you teach, Dafit. We want you to teach us, too."

It finally occurred to me that Han kept using the word we. Were there other believers in this village that I didn't know about? I was startled and confused, but excitement began crowding out these other feelings. Had God been working behind the scenes at

Kawem as He had been at Kaipom? Was He working in other villages as well? For the past few months Kaipom had seemed like one bright spot in an otherwise dark place. Was that about to change?

"Han," I ventured. "Who else in Kawem is following Jesus?"

In typical Kayagar fashion, Han used his chin to point to a group of people trailing about twenty-five feet behind us as we walked through the village.

My eyes widened and my mouth dropped as I picked out Han's two wives, his sons and daughter-in-law, his sisters, and several others I didn't recognize. I found out later that Han had been the first of this group to follow Jesus. In his role as chief of the Hahare clan, he influenced his wives to believe with him. His three sisters and two sons followed. The sisters married and their husbands believed. Tadeus, the son, married into another family. His new wife, Yuliana, believed. Then her parents and brother trusted. The trail of faith bridged from one person to another through the Hahare family and beyond.

This story repeated itself in Amaru, about one mile west of us on the Cook River and again in Amiyam, a full day's canoe trip through the rain forest to the Kronkel River. For a while it seemed as if every time I turned around someone declared faith in Christ. The tremendous feeling which began with the people movement in Kaipom swelled until it threatened to overwhelm us.

Before I could call for help, I received a radio message from John Dekker, on behalf of the Dani church. "David, the church up here in Karubaga has a young family who just completed Bible school. He's fluent in Indonesian, and both he and his wife are very intelligent. Certainly, we can use them here, but for some reason the church leaders wondered if you can use another evangelist to work with you in Kawem?"

I could only stare at the microphone in my hand. Before I had realized the need for more help, God had been preparing Lukas and Rut Kogoya. Once again God reminded us that this was His work and we could trust Him to provide all our needs. As I confirmed with John Dekker the details for Lukas joining us at Kawem, part of my mind was already working on logistical details. Where was the best village to place him? Since he spoke Indonesian so well, I would like to keep him close to me, but I didn't need an evangelist right in Kawem.

We finally decided, with the help of some of our new Christians, that Lukas and Rut should live at Amaru. He could work directly with the church in that village, pastoring the church, discipling the believers, and evangelizing the remaining unbelievers. Since Amaru was only a mile from us, he could also help at Kawem and would be close enough for us to have fellowship. He eventually became one of my best friends.

About a month later, Haram stood at the footbridge calling me and frantically waving. I ran toward the sound of his voice, "Dafit, Dafit, you must see what's happening!"

Kathy and I hurriedly followed Haram over the bridge and into the middle of Kawem. A group of men stood in the center of the path. One man leaned against a pole, his head hanging down. Haram kept up a running commentary as we approached the group. "See that man, Dafit? His family has been in debt to another one and that has caused bad feelings. Some people wanted to fight over it. Instead that man is giving his child to the other family so they can have peace. All debts will be forgiven. The child will be raised as one of their own. They will not fight as long as the child lives. Isn't that amazing?"

As the ceremony progressed, we saw the first man take his child from his wife. He held the child for all men in his family to touch, then carried the boy to the other family, where he was received in the same way. His wife stood weeping as he shuffled back to her. He turned her toward their hut, but she kept looking over her shoulder to catch another glimpse of her child.

As the crowd broke up afterward, Haram resumed his commentary. "Dafit, did you see what happened here?" He didn't give me a chance to respond before he rushed on. "There was no peace between those two families because a debt was so large it could not be repaid. People were ready to war over that debt. The only way to fix the situation was to give an innocent child. By accepting the child, this family accepted the forgiveness of the debt. The child made peace."

Haram's next words hit me with unexpected sharpness. "I know that's not exactly how you describe it, but isn't this like what God did when He offered His Son for the debt of our sins?"

I could only nod mutely.

"Couldn't you use this real-life situation to help the people here understand salvation?"

This was exactly the peace child analogy I had explained when we first arrived at Kawem. Then the Kayagar people had looked at me as though I was crazy. They couldn't seem to see the relation between their own customs and God's work. Now one of their own was explaining the analogy to me as if it were something new. Well, it was new to them. And to us it was another example of how God was moving among the Kayagar.

All through these months I was building on the foundation which had been laid just months ago in Kaipom. I taught regularly in Kawem, with frequent trips to Amaru and Kaipom. Mbitmber continued daily ministry in Kaipom. Lukas was still getting established, but teaching and preaching consistently in Amaru. Now that we were a true ministry team, we could consult, trade ideas, and make plans. One of the first things we agreed on as a team was that we still needed more help.

At the urging of Mbitmber and Lukas, I called John Dekker on the radio. Again and again he and the Dani church came to our aid. Over the next few months our ministry team grew with the addition of Nggeri Wonda and then Nggewage Wonda. Nggeri quickly established himself in the village of Amiyam on the Kronkel River. He had also ministered in the Kayagar area before our arrival, so he knew the people and language. As he began teaching at Amiyam, we saw the Lord moving there as He had within the villages closer to us. People were coming to faith in Christ.

Nggewage was new to the south coast but had pastored a church near Kanggime for several years. We needed his experience to help us organize the new churches.

Zet Hahare was a young man who helped Kathy around our house. Zet was a believer, very trustworthy and equally intelligent. After graduating from the local grade school, like all our young men, he had no place to go for either work or higher education. With the help of another missionary, we were able to help find Zet a place in a junior high school in another part of Irian Jaya. Some weeks before he was to leave, Zet came out to my office. "Bapak Dafit, I'm going to be leaving for school in Bade soon. I might not return to Kawem for three years. You know that I'm following Jesus. I would like to be baptized before I leave."

The next Sunday Zet had the distinction of being the first Kayagar baptized since our arrival. Since he worked in our house, Kathy and I had the opportunity to observe Zet's life as well as interact verbally with him. We were confident that he had trusted Christ. After our regular Sunday morning church service, I led our congregation through the village to the river, where Zet and I entered the water and I baptized him. The timing of this event was of God. By now we had enough believers in Kawem that we had begun talking about baptism. Zet was a good illustration to everyone of what was required in terms of faith and practice. I used that morning's sermon as well as Zet's testimony before his immersion to show our group what was next in their spiritual journey.

Zet was the first and last person I personally baptized. Before this I hadn't thought much about some of the secondary implications of baptism. God showed me that baptism, as an ordinance of the local church, should be administered by local church leaders. Since we didn't yet have a local church, I took that responsibility on myself for the time being.

There were, however, other possible problems. I thought about the problems the Apostle Paul wrote about in the first chapter of 1 Corinthians. It seemed, some people in the city of Corinth formed factions based on who led them to the Lord or who baptized them.

Studying this, I realized we had the seeds for the same sort of factions among the Kayagar. As wrong as it may be, the Kayagar held me in higher esteem because I was a white Westerner. I anticipated that those baptized directly by a missionary might think that baptism better than one administered by local leaders. I had to prevent that while I had the chance.

Since I had already committed myself to Zet's baptism, I went ahead with it. But I brought my problem to the evangelists and some of the more mature believers. Together we decided I shouldn't do any more baptizing, nor should I take the lead in preparing believers for baptism. God had given me a tremendous team of national evangelists who were already actively pastoring these believers. I would always be available as a resource to them, but from now on I would let these evangelists take this responsibility until we trained and appointed local leaders.

As we continued to talk and plan, Mbitmber raised a question. "Dafit, you seem to want to baptize everyone quickly. Why?"

This was a question I had already considered. "I see baptism as a sign of a believer's faith in God, not a proof of good works or a reward for living a good life. If a person truly believes in Jesus, shouldn't he be baptized immediately? I've noticed that the Indonesian church in general often waits a year or more after a person believes to baptize him. I don't think that's right." I said this with authority and thought the question was settled.

Then Mbitmber spoke. "That must work fine in the churches of your homeland, but most of these people are new to Christianity. They have no background. Our Dani tribe was once like this. Just like the Kayagar we made decisions together. Most of the time conversions were true, but sometimes a person would say the right words without understanding or truly believing.

"A few of my people were baptized, became church members, and even became leaders even though they had not personally followed Jesus. That doesn't make for a strong church. Dafit, it is better that we wait a little longer. This is not to test the believers, but to give them a chance to truly understand and affirm their decision."

I was the missionary, but I still had lessons to learn. Praise God for friends and counselors that helped me. "Your words make sense, Pendeta Mbitmber." I purposely used the honorific equivalent to Reverend to show Mbitmber I valued his wisdom. "I'll depend on you men to disciple our new believers diligently and tell me when they are ready."

The first group ready for baptism was, fittingly, in Kaipom. In January, about one year after my first exciting visit to Kaipom, I joined Mbitmber in his house to meet with ten believers.

"Esime," Mbitmber began with the first baptismal candidate, "are you following Jesus?"

"Yes, *Bapak*. I believe Jesus died to take away my sins. He is my Savior."

Mbitmber asked a few other standard questions about Esime's faith and his knowledge of basic Christian doctrine. He had the right answers, but I've never been satisfied with just hearing the right answers. I wanted to know Esime's own thoughts in his own words, so I interjected a leading question.

"Why do you want to be baptized, Esime?"

The poor guy looked stunned. He had prepared answers for many questions, but this was not one of them. He looked from my face to Mbitmber's, then responded, "I believe Jesus died to take away my sins."

"Yes, you already said that and it makes me happy. But why do you want to be baptized?"

I knew that I was asking something difficult. Not that the answer in itself is that difficult, but the question was an unusual one for this culture. Tribal people often have trouble thinking in the abstract. They are much more comfortable when they have a specific correct answer to a specific question, and that answer is either right or wrong.

I pressed, "Esime, I know that you are a true follower of Jesus. I see that by your life. I'm not here to test your faith. I just want to hear you tell me what's in your heart. Don't worry about the words. Just tell me why you want to be baptized."

"For a long time our people did not know anything about the true God. When you came here I heard there is a God we can know. That God is concerned about my life and wants to help me. I was in the house right over there when you asked us if we would follow Jesus. I joined the other men in saying 'yes,' because in my heart I knew that it was the right thing to do for our people and for me as one man. I promised I would learn God's Word from His book and try to live so He will be happy with my life. His book tells me I should be baptized, so I will.

"There is another reason. Many of our people from other villages are not following Jesus. They look at us and wonder if this is real. When I am baptized in this river I want them all to see and know that I belong to Jesus. Sometimes our people don't believe our words. If they see my actions, they will know this is true. Maybe then they will believe, too."

What could I add to that? Esime had caught the essence of baptism: obedience to and identification with Christ.

On January 8, 1977, I stood on the banks of the Cook River with hundreds of people from the Autohoim and Kayagar tribes. Together we watched the birth of a new church as Mbitmber baptized nine people from Kaipom. It's hard to call nine people a "mass," but as far as I know, that was the first mass believers' baptism to ever take place in either of these two tribal groups.

Ten days later the scene was repeated at Amiyam where Nggeri and Mbitmber baptized nineteen believers. Two weeks later Lukas oversaw the baptism of fifteen Christians in Amaru. It is ironic that the village closest to the missionary was the last one ready, but two days later Lukas and Mbitmber baptized eighteen people in Kawem. We still weren't finished. Kaipom had nineteen more believers ready to publicly declare their faith by the end of February.

God added and multiplied in front of our eyes. From a tribe with practically no Christian knowledge, God moved across rain forest and river to redeem hundreds. We jumped from no organized churches to four. Our leadership swelled from two workers—Kathy and me—to a ministry team of seven families when the Dani evangelists and teachers joined us. God strengthened the faith of each leader and follower through these experiences.

CHAPTER SEVEN APPLICATION GUIDE

"Now faith is being sure of what we hope for and certain of what we do not see" Hebrews 11:1 (NIV).

God gives faith deep in our hearts and changes our whole lives. A change in our belief system results in a change in our thoughts, a change in our thoughts results in different words and actions. True living faith will show in our actions. "In the same way, faith by itself, if it is not accompanied by action, is dead" James 2:17 (NIV).

Dave and Kathy saw examples of how God gave faith to the people of Irian Jaya, and how this faith worked itself out in their lives. Their thought processes changed, and their actions changed. They truly became new creations.

If Dave had tried to change the Kayagar people's actions, he would have met with strong resistance. Through faith, God made the changes deep within the people's hearts; and their desires changed. Dave could simply watch God do His work and rejoice. Being God's co-worker is the way to go!

We can't focus on our faith; we must focus on the object of our faith—God. For He is the only trustworthy One. Faith in God is essential to our salvation. "And without faith it is impossible to please God, because anyone who comes to him must believe that he exists and that he rewards those who earnestly seek him" Hebrews 11:6 (NIV).

Faith results in more prayer, and prayer results in more faith. What a great circle of blessing we can enter into through faith.

PONDER these Scriptures:

Luke 17:5-6; Galatians 2:20;
Ephesians 2:8-9.

PRAISE God for His faithfulness.

Think about God's unchanging commitment toward you.

Read these verses in praise to God: Psalm 89:1-2, 8; Psalm 92:1-2.

PEER into your heart.

Has God given you faith?

Are you exercising it?

PRAYER

Faithful Father, I praise You because You are trustworthy. Thank You for placing faith in my heart. I want to exercise my faith in You. Please give me opportunities to do this. Forgive me for not praying in faith more often. Please help me encourage others faithfully. Bless the missionaries who have stepped out in faith to share Your word. Plant faith in the heart of unbelievers and help them learn to rely on You. I pray in Jesus' Name. Amen.

CHAPTER EIGHT

God Gives Life

"Don't go so fast, Art," I squeaked. After living at sea level for over a year, now climbing this mountain at 8,000 feet, squeaking was the best I could do.

Kathy and I had come to Ninia, in the eastern highlands, to visit RBMU missionaries, Art and Carol Clark. This was our first real vacation since arriving in Kawem. I didn't know what was in store when Art said, "Would you like to take a walk with me today?" Pointing at the mountain range in back of his house, he said, "Let's aim for that peak."

We quickly lost sight of that peak as we trekked up the winding path, worn by thousands of bare feet walking this path through the centuries. The air became cooler and thinner as we moved steadily higher.

We passed a couple of men digging with long pointed sticks. In this culture, the men prepare the ground and the women plant, tend, and harvest the sweet potatoes. The men had pig grease smeared over their bodies, and when they worked up a sweat, they smelled a little like spoiled bacon cooking. They were naked except for hair nets and the long yellow gourds they wore in place of loincloths. These bright gourds, nearly two feet long, accented their nakedness to those of us who weren't used to seeing this type of "dress," yet the tribesmen from the highlands considered them more modest than our clothing.

We waved and continued on a couple of hundred feet until we came to a crest with a beautiful view. We took a welcome break and sat in silence eating sandwiches, drinking water from our canteens, and marveling at the endless range of mountains.

Every time we topped one rise, we found another beyond it—all standing in the way of our final goal. Quite often I found myself wanting to ask like a child, "Are we almost there?"

Finally, we reached our goal. "It took longer than I thought," Art said, "but we made it."

Hands on my knees, trying to catch my breath, I glanced at Art and gasped, "Man, you set me up! I never dreamed it was this far, but it did give me time to think.

"Here we walked over rise after rise before getting to the top. This is what we're going through in the ministry at Kawem right now. We struggled up the mountain of evangelism and found discipleship waiting. We tackled that, with the help of our Dani evangelists, and we moved on to baptism. Now we've reached the challenge of church organization.

"Art, when we called you a few weeks ago, Kathy and I knew we needed a rest. I didn't expect to spend much time thinking about Kawem, but you and Carol have given us the chance to reflect on what we left behind and what's waiting for us. In fact, this little walk has really helped me put things in perspective. I think we'll be more than ready to get home when the plane comes for us in a few days. Thanks."

The goal Kathy and I always kept in mind was establishing self-supporting, self-governing, and self-reproducing local churches. By its most basic definition, a local church requires nothing more than a group of believers. These believers, however, need leaders. Ideally, these leaders come from within the group, and the people support them.

The day we moved to Kawem, Haram had introduced us to the church and its leaders. "Follow me," Haram called to the small group of people waiting at our door. He led them into our living room. He addressed me more formally than usual, "Tuan Dafit, here is your church. These are the people Tuan John baptized before you came here." He introduced each person by name. "I am the elder in charge of all the believers. Hainam is the elder at Amaru. Waipe is the elder in Kawem. Palu is an assistant elder."

I looked again at the group. There were four men and two women. Every man had a leadership position in the church. The only people they had to lead were the two women.

"Aren't there any others, Haram?"

"No, these are all the baptized believers in these two villages."

I saw at least two challenges waiting for us. The first was bringing in new believers. The second was building a leadership structure.

I realized people had been placed in leadership positions with little understanding of what those offices meant. Haram was a natural leader and strong Christian. Though untrained, he functioned as head elder and was taking his responsibilities seriously. Others, though, saw their offices or titles as a matter of prestige rather than calling, honor instead of responsibility. As the church grew over the next year, it became obvious some new believers would be better qualified to lead the church than leaders already in place. But how could I make such a transition?

Badly, as it turned out.

Kawem and Amaru were the only villages with any formal church structure at this point. I decided it would be better to reorganize now. Struck with awe, I looked at the many new believers from Amaru and Kawem after the first round of baptisms. "It's time for me to begin teaching you about becoming a church. Because God has started a new work here, we're also going to start all things new. I will be the elder for all of the churches while I teach you about the responsibilities of leadership. Next year each church can choose its own elders from among those who have been trained."

Most of them looked attentive and accepted this announcement, but it was obvious Waipe had something he wanted to say. He was one of the former elders I had just replaced with myself. He was a good but young man, with too high an opinion of himself. There is a reason the Bible cautions against placing a young man or new believer into leadership, and Waipe was an example of this. He had potential, but was not ready for the responsibilities of leadership. I hoped he would understand all of this.

As we exited the Kawem church building, Waipe dashed to my side and pulled me away from the others. "Dafit, I didn't quite understand what you just did in church. You made yourself an elder?"

"That's right, Waipe. With so many new Christians, we all need some time to get to know one another and grow so we can agree on new elders."

"But I'm still an elder, right?"

"No. I explained that it's best for all elders to step down so we can start new."

"But, Dafit," Waipe strengthened the tone of his voice, "I want to be an elder. Tuan John told me I was an elder before you came here. Who are you to take this privilege away from me?"

"Waipe, you're my brother in Christ. I'm glad you're here to help. But God is giving us many new brothers in Christ. Some of them might be better qualified than you to..." As soon as I spoke those words, I knew I had said the wrong thing.

Before I could even try to rephrase my words, Waipe shouted, "What do you mean better qualified than I am? I have been a Christian longer than all of them. I was in this church before you were here. I'm important! If you don't want me, then I'll just leave." Off he stormed.

I had made a major mistake and knew it, but there was little I could do to correct it immediately. From experience, I knew it was best to give Waipe time to cool his temper.

For now, I had to settle in my own mind how a church should be organized. Ultimately, I wanted a team of elders to share pastoral and teaching ministries. Since I grew up in a democratic society, I was used to choosing leaders through elections and assumed this was the best way. It might well be the best way in our North American culture, but it was a far cry from the way people in Irian Jaya chose leaders.

The Kayagar did not elect anyone to anything. They set leadership patterns in advance and most positions came by heredity.

Shortly after baptizing the first thirteen people at Kaipom, I let the new church choose their own leadership. I wasn't sure how to organize a church, and I decided to try what seemed best and change if it didn't work. They chose Au as their one elder.

He was unqualified by my standards. Though Au and his wife, Kipi, were among the first baptized believers in Kaipom, he was illiterate. "It's good to see our children and young men going to school," Au explained to us. "I am too old to do that. I just can't do that."

At forty, Au was almost a senior citizen in a society where the average life span might be in the early fifties. He seemed set in his ways and uncomfortable with new situations. He wasn't part of the tribal leadership structure, and I didn't know him well enough to recognize his potential.

When I questioned the church's decision, people spoke up, "Au has changed since he began following Jesus. We have seen a difference in his life. He understands God's ways."

Who was I to argue? That was a better reason than I had sometimes heard in North American churches. "Okay, great," I said. "Au is your new elder."

One day soon after he became a church leader, Au brought his wife, Kipi, to the clinic.

Kathy told me they were waiting, then added, "Kipi must really be sick for them to paddle two hours to get to the clinic, and Au is carrying their baby. That's not normal."

"That's right," I responded. "Every time I've seen them in the village, the baby has been in Kipi's arms, with other children following close behind her."

"Dafid, Kipi is sick. What can you do for her?" Au asked.

Her grass skirt rustled as she walked slowly toward me. Her face looked gaunt and her eyes dull. I spread out a grass mat and helped Kipi to a sitting position. "How do you feel?" I asked.

Au translated her answers into Indonesian because Kipi only spoke their tribal language. "Hot," was her answer.

"Do you hurt any place?"

She groaned, and Au said, "She told me this morning she hurts everywhere."

I noticed Au was more attentive to Kipi than most tribal men were to their wives. I took her temperature and she had a slight fever, but I couldn't find anything else obviously wrong. I wasn't too concerned because various fevers were common. I gave her some aspirin for the fever and a shot of penicillin to fight any infection she might have. Then I told Au to take her home and let her rest.

Within two days Kipi died.

I was shaken to the core as a missionary and hurt for them as their friend. Needing some counsel, I walked to Haram's house. "*Yahanap*, you know that Au's wife has died." Talking to myself as much as Au, I continued, "This was the first death in the village since they committed themselves to the Lord. Kipi herself was a baptized believer. She was the wife of a church leader. Haram, how do you think the people of Kaipom will respond? How will her death affect the people's faith? Will they be angry with God or with me?"

"Those people in Kaipom think differently than we do, Dafit. I could tell you what my people would do, but I don't know how Au and his people will react."

Though only ten miles separated the two villages in space, language and culture separated them in other ways. Once more, the reality of life in the rain forest showed its impact.

I couldn't go to Kaipom because my outboard motor was broken; I would have to wait and see how Kipi's death affected them.

It was almost a week before we saw Au again. When he came across our yard, I sped to him and embraced him. We shared a moment of sorrow. As I stepped back to look closely at his face, I was startled to see how Au was smiling.

"Dafid, let me tell you what happened in our village."

I stared in amazement; this is not the response I had expected.

He continued, "When Kipi died, everybody in the village prepared for the big feast we normally have. We always carry the body of a dead person into the forest. You know we don't have a lot of dry land to bury our dead as some do. Instead, we put the bodies in the trees. Then we return to the village and make a lot of noise. That scares the departed spirit into the forest so it won't haunt us.

"I felt uncomfortable about what we were doing but did not know why. Some of the men helped me lift Kipi's body. As we did that, I seemed to hear a voice behind me say, 'You shouldn't do this now that you're a Christian.' I turned to look, but there was no one there, but now I knew why I did not feel at peace.

"I looked across my wife's body at the other men and said, 'I don't think this is the right thing to do because we are now Christians.' They agreed but waited for me to direct them."

"'You are our elder,' they said. 'Tell us what to do.'"

"The evangelist, Mbitmber, taught us we could ask God for wisdom, so I prayed quickly, '*Tuan Yesus*, tell me what to do.' So many thoughts crowded into my head, what will happen to Kipi's spirit? What will happen to us if we offend God? I did not know the answer to the questions, but I knew I could not continue with this ceremony until I talked to Mbitmber.

"Since Mbitmber had gone to visit another village, I left my infant daughter with relatives and walked all night through the forest until I found him. He came back with me the next day.

"As Mbitmber saw the group of men watching for our return, he ran ahead of me. 'Friends, I have more good news for you. Kipi is not here!' he shouted.

"One of the men replied, 'No, she is dead.'

"Mbitmber turned to him and smiled. 'The Bible teaches us that the spirit of a believer doesn't roam the forest or stay in the village. It goes immediately to live with *Tuan Yesus*.'

"I felt comforted by those words," said Au. "I don't understand everything Mbitmber said that day, but I believe it is true.

"Dafe, I don't know if you ever do this in your country, but is it good to hold a service in the church even when it's not Sunday? Could you come down to our village and talk with us about Kipi's death?"

He was asking me to perform a memorial service. I was almost too stunned to speak. No one had ever taught him that; he just thought it was the right thing to do.

"I can do that, Au. When would you like me to come to Kaipom?"

Pointing to his canoe, he replied, "The church is full. They are waiting for you now."

I had barely enough time to grab my Bible. "Kathy," I yelled as I raced through the house. She came running from the room in which she'd been working, and I quickly explained the situation. Soon I was watching Au's lean muscles tighten as he paddled the canoe swiftly down the river.

Two hours later we rounded a bend in the Cook River and Kaipom village became visible. What I saw forced me to my feet, balancing precariously in the rocking canoe. "Where did all those people come from? Au..." I couldn't even finish my sentence. I could only stare.

Even from the canoe, I could see more people standing outside the church building than lived in the entire village. As we paddled closer, I saw that the church itself was packed with even more people.

"I forgot to tell you, Dafit, that the people who live downriver want to hear what you will say, too."

That was an understatement. There were three more Autohoim villages further east on the Cook River. No one in those villages had yet trusted Christ, and they had been very vocal in their opposition to what was happening in Kaipom. Walking to the church, I picked up bits of their whispered conversations. "There he is," they pointed at me with their chins. "What will he say?" one man wondered aloud.

"What can he say?" another challenged. "He promised eternal life and someone has died. He has lied to these people."

"That's right! He said his God was more powerful than the spirits. We know sickness is caused by the spirits. Obviously his God can't even protect His own people!"

The hair stood up on my neck as I realized what was going on around me. These non-believers were trying to reinforce their opposition and draw the people of Kaipom back to the old ways. They had grabbed onto Kipi's death in an attempt to demonstrate that the ancestral spirits were stronger than the new God of Kaipom.

I saw clearly what had to happen this afternoon. I had to comfort the believers, and more importantly reinforce their faith. I also had to give a strong and positive testimony to those who opposed the gospel. As my mind raced, it kept coming back to the biblical passage God had impressed on my heart over the past several weeks.

Kornelius stood by to translate my Indonesian words into Autohoim as I opened my Bible to Revelation chapter five, verse nine. I read the words John recorded on the Island of Patmos. John was experiencing a vision of heaven, seeing God on the throne. He saw Jesus as the sacrificial Lamb of God. He heard the elders sing a new song to the Lamb.

> You are worthy to take the scroll
> and to open its seals,
> because you were slain,
> and with your blood you purchased men for God
> *from every tribe, and language, and people, and nation.*

I waited for Kornelius to translate before I continued, "Until this week, there has never been a representative from this village who stood face-to-face with Jesus. Today, Kipi is there!" I stopped.

For a brief moment, the church was so quiet I could hear the wind gently blowing through the thatch roof. Suddenly, it seemed as if every person there began talking at the same time.

"Did you hear what he said?" someone asked aloud.

"Did he say Kipi is in heaven?" another shouted.

"Kipi, our own Kipi?"

"She was living with us last week and now she's living in heaven with Jesus?"

Even the non-Christians were saying, "Is that true?"

I watched in awe as something I could not explain ran through the crowd. What began as questions and statements of doubt were changing to shouts of joy and triumph. I watched eyes filled with sorrow brighten as if a lamp had been turned on behind them.

"It must be true," Au shouted. "Kipi is with Jesus. My Kipi—our Kipi—is in heaven!"

I didn't understand what was happening, even though I was thrilled with the results.

Later, I learned the people of this culture have a mental map which is bounded by their group experiences. Only places they know and have visited are on that map. But they do have a way to add new points to the map. It didn't seem logical to me, but they explained that if someone from their own people goes to a place outside of those boundaries, even if that person never comes back to report about it, they believe that place exists.

In their minds, on that day, heaven became a real place—as real as their own village. They already knew two people there now—Jesus and their own Kipi.

Even the unbelievers had to rethink their opposition. Their own cultural logic now told them this faith was trustworthy.

What I was afraid would destroy the faith of the young church had built their faith even stronger. Through their few months of following Christ, they had believed even when they didn't understand. Now, in a way I couldn't explain, God had given them understanding, using their own cultural beliefs that were more real to them than any illustration I could have given. Excited, they drew together in celebration. Because of the growth and testimony of this village, other villages along the river started opening up to the gospel message.

CHAPTER EIGHT APPLICATION GUIDE

"Flesh gives birth to flesh, but the Spirit gives birth to spirit" John 3:6 (NIV).

Dave and Art saw men preparing ground for planting seeds. We can see many illustrations of how God gives spiritual life through observing how He gives life in gardens. I notice four steps:

1) **Prepare ground.** How can we prepare the ground of human hearts to receive the seed of God's Word? What hardens hearts? Hurt causes a callous to form. What softens hearts? Prayer and forgiveness. Ask yourself: Do I need to make a relationship right? Is my pride keeping someone else's heart hard so the Word of God won't take root?
2) **Plant seeds.** Share the pure Word of God, persistently bathed in prayer. "When anyone hears the message about the kingdom and does not understand it, the evil one comes and snatches away what was sown in his heart..." Matthew 13:19 (NIV).
3) **Protect plants.** Young plants especially need care and protection. According to the parable of the sower, "The one who received the seed [of God's Word] that fell among the thorns is the man who hears the word, but the worries of this life and the deceitfulness of wealth choke it, making it unfruitful" Matthew 13:22 (NIV).
4) **Provide nourishment.** Jesus said, "I am the true vine, and my Father is the gardener" John 15:1 (NIV). "I am the vine; you are the branches. If a man remains in me and I in him, he will bear much fruit; apart from me you can do nothing" John 15:5 (NIV). We get our nourishment from clinging to Jesus and drawing from His attributes.

PONDER these Scriptures:

Romans 6:1-11; Colossians 2:8-13; Ephesians 2:1-10.

PRAISE God for life.

"For in him we live and move and have our being..." Acts 17:28 (NIV).

Think about how dependent we are on God and what He has given us.

PEER into your heart.

Has God given you new life in Christ?

Are your earthly desires dead? (Read Colossians 3.)

PRAYER

Life-giving Father, I praise You for everlasting spiritual life. Thank You for every heartbeat and every breath of my physical life. I want to live in a way that glorifies You. Please help me labor in prayer for the new life of others. Help missionaries around the world as they explain salvation to unbelievers. Open spiritual eyes so they can see Your truths and receive eternal life. I ask this in the Name of Jesus, the way, the truth, and the life. Amen.

CHAPTER NINE

God Gives Light

I woke with a start! What was it that woke me? After our months living in Kawem, I should have been familiar with the night sounds. Yet, sometimes, as on nights like this, it all seemed new and somewhat menacing. As I lay in the dark room, sleep eluded me, and imagination ran free. I listened to the soft breathing of my wife and daughter, for whom I carried a feeling of responsibility. However, strange smells and noises propelled my mind into a realm where I was once again a child afraid of the dark. Animal sounds bounced through the air daring me to recognize them and feel more at ease; but I couldn't. Unseen night creatures scurried here and there. The leathery flapping of bats' wings drifted from our fruit trees. And all the while, drums beat steadily in the background. The darkness brought with it a helpless, hopeless feeling.

Then, as if the clock began racing ahead, a small ray of light appeared through the window. Tree branches cast their cryptic shadows across the room. Suddenly, the sun burst fully into view, pushing aside the darkness as though it were nothing.

Light! It brought confidence and hope. After moving to Irian Jaya where reaching for a light switch was not an option, I appreciated light more. No wonder God's Word describes Jesus as the Light of the world.

Before we went to Kawem, people told us we would probably want a generator—and they were right. We were thankful for our kerosene pump lamps, but we knew how much a generator would enhance our lives. We began researching what other missionaries were using, pricing generators, and getting permission to raise support to buy one. We had brought some wiring and electrical supplies with us because we knew eventually we wanted to go in that direction. After awhile we found a new brand of generator from Japan, smaller and less expensive than the ones from Germany most others were using, and I sent a letter to Eddie Susanto, the purchasing agent in the capital city asking him to order one from Japan. Eddie radioed to ask if there was a special reason I wanted him to order it, because they sold them in town cheaper. Thrilled, I gave him the go-ahead to buy a Yanmar generator and store it in the MAF warehouse until we found a way to get it home.

Paul Kline was a missionary who could fix anything. He blessed many people when he joined our mission team as a technical support specialist. We invited Paul and his family to stay with us for a few days while he wired the house properly and set up the generator. They came within the week after Kristen was born.

The Cook River rose and fell with the seasons. Now, in the middle of the dry season, it was at such a low level that the MAF floatplane couldn't land in front of our house. I had to pick up Paul and his family by canoe at a nearby village. Pilot Joe Hoisington didn't like landing there either; though the water was higher, he didn't have a very long straight stretch of river. He told me he wouldn't come down there again if he could help it. But since we had no other way to get a generator, he agreed to give it a try.

Joe returned to his base and measured the generator so I would know how big a canoe to bring. We arranged to meet at the same place, since it still seemed the best option. The day he was to come, I paddled down there and waited. His plane passed by several times, then he opened the window and yelled above the noise of the engine, "Water's too low. Can't come in." I could barely make out his words before the plane disappeared. After about an hour, I realized he wasn't coming back. I paddled back home wondering if we would have electricity in the near future.

When I got home, the generator was there. Joe had landed close to our house after all, and Paul had already installed it. After that, we used electricity about two hours each night and for special occasions, such as using power tools.

Though light seemed important to us, the Kayagar people were happy as they were. They weren't convinced they wanted change, and they didn't envy us for having electricity.

Many Kayagar people had the same attitude about spiritual light. It was fine for us, but they didn't see a need for Jesus in their own lives. The Kayagar were animists. They believed virtually every physical object in the world had a spirit or spiritual force within it. Kathy and I had learned this as theory in college. Now we saw the consequences of lives based on this belief.

The Bible does teach about spiritual forces at work in the world. Just as Jesus confronted personal demons, many of the ills of our world could be the direct result of such beings. We hadn't thought much about spiritual warfare since our Western worldview generally ignores anything that can't be seen or measured in a scientific way. Living with the Kayagar culture and worldview, Kathy and I began to examine and evaluate our own culture.

"Dave, are you home?" After living with only the Kayagar and my family for the past six months, it felt strange to hear a male voice call my name in English. Steve Knapp was a student from Talbot Seminary who worked with us that summer. He continued, "My friends will expect me to bring home some primitive artifacts. Can you get your people to bring in some things I can buy as souvenirs?"

I spread the word that Steve wanted to buy some artifacts and people should bring things they wanted to sell. Among those who responded to this call was Hani, from the village of Airo, who brought a fancy headdress which fit over the entire head. It had cowrie shells sewn in it and the grass equivalent of dreadlocks falling to the sides. It was very unique and attractive. Steve liked it and bought it for the equivalent of a few U.S. dollars, but later he questioned his decision. "Dave, I haven't seen any other headdresses like this one. Do you know anything about when it is worn and why?

"No, Steve. I haven't seen anything like that either."

When Haram came over next I passed the question along to him. "What's the significance of this headdress?"

Haram smiled. "This can only be made and worn by a warrior who has killed another man."

Steve's face paled.

"The man who made this caught his wife in adultery and killed both her and her lover. He made the headdress so everyone would know that he is a strong man and not afraid to kill when provoked. He used some materials from the possessions of the man he killed, so the strength of that man is captured in the headdress."

Hearing the story, Steve decided he didn't really want that artifact. Neither of us understood all the spiritual implications, but I kept the headdress. I needed more understanding of the animist mind before I gave up my Western skepticism.

"Hermanus," I called to one of the young believers of Kawem. I thought I could turn this into a teaching moment. "Before you were a believer and before there was a clinic here, did your child ever get sick?"

"Oh yes," he responded and began telling me how Damaris almost died from a fever.

"I see that Damaris is still here. Did you ask the spirits for help?"

Hermanus was embarrassed to speak about the subject and looked down at the ground, a cultural signal that I shouldn't go into this area. I didn't pick up on his signal, so I repeated the question and expanded on it. "What did you do the get the spirits' help?"

After some time, he responded, "Dafit, we thought Damaris would die. She wouldn't eat sago or even nurse from her mother. Her skin was so hot we cut holes for the sickness to escape, but it didn't. Finally I took some gifts to the spirit who controls sickness. I took a bow, arrows, and some fish line. I carried those things to the *aitn* where the spirit lives and left them as gifts for the spirit. The next day Damaris was well."

Thinking to show Hermanus that he was mistaken, I asked, "What about the bow and fish line you left for the spirit? Was it gone from the *aitn*?"

"No," he answered immediately. "I went back the next day and took it."

"There!" I almost shouted. "If the spirit was so strong, why didn't it take the gifts you left?" With my Western logic I tried to show him that if the spirit could not take the gifts, it certainly couldn't have affected Damaris' health.

Kayagar culture didn't allow him to argue about it. Hermanus' only response was a weak, "Yes, you are probably right."

Later when I had a better understanding of animistic belief, I came back to him and said, "Hermanus, do you remember when we talked about Damaris' sickness and the spirit who helped make her well?"

Of course he remembered, but he wasn't going to answer until he saw where I was taking this conversation.

"I think I was wrong when I talked to you about that." My words obviously took him by surprise, so I continued quickly. "Then I thought the spirit wasn't strong because it didn't take the gifts you left."

Hermanus nodded to show that he was listening.

"Now I think 'what good are physical gifts to a spirit?' Could it be that the spirit took the *mana* or spiritual power out of your gifts and left the physical part behind?"

Hermanus looked at me with respectful awe. "Dafit, you're beginning to understand."

During our days at Bible college, in our missionary training, and in the North American church in general, spiritual warfare was virtually ignored. That left Kathy and me very unprepared to understand or respond to the situation in which we found ourselves. We came to believe there was real demonic activity and true spiritual warfare, but we didn't know how to deal with it.

Though it took years, I was beginning to realize how deeply animism touched the entire life of a Kayagar. The spirits were in a precarious balance with the physical world. As long as the spirits were content, they wouldn't tip the balance of nature or do direct harm to a living person. Much of Kayagar life, then, was spent in keeping the spirits happy so that the Kayagar, in turn, could live trouble-free lives. If the Kayagar life and culture was held together in balance by appeasing the spirit world, change of any sort was to be avoided. Safety lay in following the *rules* of life, laid down by centuries of tradition.

"Why do you do this?" I asked a man from Amaru who was carving a spirit pole.

"My father did it like this," was the reply.

"Why did he do that?"

"His father did it before him."

I stopped there, because I knew we could keep that exchange going for hours.

As I gained spiritual insight, I looked for more opportunities to interact with the Kayagar about the supernatural. I often used canoe trips as an excuse to build relationships. By hiring men to paddle my canoe, I could spend several uninterrupted hours talking with them. Such an opportunity came when the village of Ahmwi moved from its location in the rain forest to a new site next to Kawem. There was no great material advantage to their move, so I wondered if they had a spiritual reason. I soon found an excuse to travel by canoe and asked some men from Ahmwi to paddle.

"Notm," I called to the paddler nearest me in the long canoe. "You've heard me talking about God's power, and you seem interested. Why don't you become a Christian?"

"You should not ask a question like that, Dafit. If you were one of my children I would say be patient, and you will understand after many years. Since you are not like us, I will answer you. We are comfortable and set in our ways. We must have balance in our lives. The spirits are happy, nature is happy, and we are happy. If we change anything, we might upset this balance. That is why we always do the same thing the same way throughout our lives.

"Now you come here with something so new it cannot help but change our lives. If we change, the spirits will no longer be happy. Nature will no longer be happy. That means we would no longer be happy. You say that your God is strong enough to protect us, but we do not know that. How can we trust something we do not know? It is better to stay with our familiar ways."

By this time I knew enough not to argue with him, but I did want to leave a seed for thought. After all, he and his entire village had taken the initiative to physically move closer to the gospel. There was a glimmer of light peeking through the darkness of his world.

"Notm, my friend." I chose my words carefully to encourage the light. "There are already whole families in Kawem and other villages who have believed in Jesus. You've seen that their lives continue. Change is coming, my friend."

Notm didn't answer. I said no more, but I prayed God would nurture the seed I had planted in his heart.

The people of Ahmwi had come from upriver. Light was also dawning in the downriver village of Airo. This was actually a collection of three smaller villages which had moved together in a central spot on the river. In times past, the Kayagar had been semi-nomadic. The groupings we called villages were little more than extended families traveling together for mutual protection.

Over time, the Indonesian government exerted more influence over tribal life. For administrative purposes they encouraged families and villages to move together in central locations. Even when they did come together, each village established its own recognized boundaries. What outsiders saw as one physical village could actually be several clans. In the case of Airo, I quickly learned there were three villages there, but I never figured out which was which.

After Kipi's funeral, we sensed that some families in Airo were becoming interested in the gospel. About the same time the Ministry of Education placed an evangelical Christian as a teacher in the public school there. Guru Gobay was the first real witness within the village. Gobay and his family began spending much of their free time with our teachers and evangelists and became frequent visitors at Kawem.

"*Selamat siang*, Tuan Dafit." I looked up from the outboard motor I was cleaning to see Gobay standing a few feet away.

"*Selamat siang*, Pak Guru. How are you this afternoon?" I asked. We had begun the necessary preliminaries to a real conversation. All told we would spend ten to twenty minutes exchanging polite small talk before getting to the real reason for his visit.

"Tuan, since my family moved into Airo, we have felt the lack of close fellowship. We have spent much time with the teachers you placed in the Christian villages, but we have to travel an hour or more to visit any fellow believers. Last month we began a church in our own house. At first just my wife and I met, but over the past weeks some others have begun meeting with us."

Gobay had found me in one of my cautious moods. Alarm bells went off in my head. "You're new to this area, Guru Gobay," I began, "so you might not understand some of the difficulties we face here.

"The local government has determined that each village should have only one religion. They are afraid there would be rivalry and even fighting within the villages if there is more than one religion represented there. Even before we came to this area, the unwritten rule has been that once a group chooses to follow a religion, other religious groups may not interfere with them or seek to convert the people."

I was trying to express my understanding of local politics in the least offensive way. Indonesian law guarantees freedom of religion. Everyone is free to belong to one of the five official religions: Buddhism, Hinduism, Islam, Catholicism, or Protestantism. Animism is not recognized by the Indonesian government as a true religion. By the time we arrived in Kawem, most villages were designated as either Catholic or Protestant, seen as two separate faiths. As far as we could see among the Kayagar, Catholicism was little more than a label which added some Christian terminology, but allowed all of the old animistic belief and practice.

"I am pleased to hear about your church, Pak Guru, but I'm not sure what I can do to help you. Airo is a Catholic village." I don't think I was making excuses, just describing the situation as I understood it.

"Tuan Dafit, you aren't listening to me." Gobay was speaking forcefully as if teaching civics to a class full of students. "I am an Indonesian citizen. I have the freedom to choose my religion. I have chosen to be a Protestant. I have the right to worship, even if it's only in my own home. When my family began worshipping in Airo, some people joined us of their own will. These people are asking you, through me, to come to our village and teach us from God's Word."

Now he had my full attention and I saw the implications of this conversation. Gobay and his "church" were inviting me to preach the gospel in a closed village. A few days later I visited Gobay in his home at Airo. He had arranged to have the village chief and other leaders present.

"I'm honored to be invited to Guru Gobay's home today. I'm also pleased that he has invited you so we can get to know one another." Discussions like this take time in the Indonesian and tribal contexts. We spent the next hour in small talk. The second hour went by as we reviewed tradition, history, and government policies regarding religion.

The village chief brought the discussion to a head. "I don't understand why you are here, Tuan Dafit. We already have a religion. We are registered as a Catholic village. We have a church and a religious teacher. You should not be here trying to change that."

"I respect your choice, *Kepala* (chief)," I responded politely. One of my greatest problems has always been impatience. I was fighting to control myself and be polite, yet I wanted to move the conversation in a different direction. "I am not trying to change your ways unless you also want that, but I would like to ask what you do believe."

That was not a question he expected. Caught off guard, he replied, "We have the same words as you. We have the same book as you."

"That's good to hear, Kepala. Have you read that book?"

"No," he admitted. "But we have the book."

I had seen this before among tribal peoples in Irian Jaya and had studied the phenomena in other parts of the world. Having the book was more important than knowing what it said. Without proper understanding, the Bible became little more than another magic charm added to animistic faith. It was a way of merging Christianity with the belief system they already held. They were more comfortable with this and felt it maintained balance in the spiritual world.

Realizing he was losing control of the conversation, the chief sought to reestablish himself. "We have the right to choose our religion. We have chosen to be Catholic. You are not permitted to question our ways or force your ways on us. We don't want you in our village."

"I also have freedom of religion, Kepala," Gobay broke into the flow. "Tuan Dafit and I respect you and your choice, but you must respect mine. I am a Protestant. I choose to worship as a Protestant, even if it is in my own home. If I choose to invite Tuan Dafit or one of the evangelists to visit and worship in my home, that is my right. If others choose to join me, that is their right as Indonesian citizens. Kepala, you are an officer of our Indonesian government. Your duty is to enforce the law, even if you don't agree with it. I call on you as chief of this village to give us our rights."

That all but ended the discussion. We now had the seeds of a church in Airo. Gobay pulled me aside to talk privately just before I left to return to Kawem. "Don't be disappointed by our talks today," he cautioned me. "We few believers will be faithful and draw others to us."

Gobay was focusing on the opposition to the gospel. I was already thinking past this day. The people of this village had been living in darkness for centuries, even after the light of the gospel was available to them. True, this was not a movement as we had seen in Kaipom; the numbers were relatively few. But the darkness was no longer complete. Spiritual dawn was breaking, and nothing would stop God's light from penetrating Airo.

CHAPTER NINE APPLICATION GUIDE

"This is the verdict: Light has come into the world, but men loved darkness instead of light because their deeds were evil. Everyone who does evil hates the light, and will not come into the light for fear that his deeds will be exposed. But whoever lives by the truth comes into the light, so that it may be seen plainly that what he has done has been done through God" John 3:19-21 (NIV).

In heaven, there will be no need for the sun because God's glory will supply all the light we need. To those of us who walk in spiritual light, this thought is warm and comforting. Light guides us and protects us from harm. Yet, if all we have ever known is darkness, light can be frightening. It reveals our weaknesses.

I thought my kitchen was clean until the bright sun shone through the windows, revealing spots on the stove, flaws in the table, and dust floating through the air. I was more comfortable before I saw this. Once I thought I was a good person and rationalized my wrong actions. Then God's light shone on my heart, revealing my selfishness and sins. I was more comfortable before I saw this, yet I needed to see the truth so I could turn to Christ for cleansing.

The Kayagar people were comfortable in their spiritual blindness and sins. They were afraid of the unknown. They didn't want to face the truth, because that would mean sorrow and repentance (turning around and going the other way). It was easier to rationalize (rational lies) their way of life.

God's light pushes away the darkness. They cannot co-exist.

PONDER these Scriptures:

Psalm 119:106; Isaiah 60:1-2,19; John 1:1-13;

I John 1:5-10.

PRAISE God for light.

Think what your life would be without light.

Read Psalm 104:1-3 aloud as praise to God.

PEER into your heart.

Are you more comfortable in darkness or the light of God's Word?

Are you walking in the light of God?

PRAYER

Father of Light, I praise You for Your radiance. Thank You for giving me spiritual light so I can see my need for You. I pray for those who have never seen Your light or heard about Your love. Please send laborers to these unreached people to give them light and hope. Help me shine with Your light so others will see You in me. I pray in the Name of Jesus, Light of the world. Amen.

CHAPTER TEN

God Gives Grace

I followed the crowd rushing to the riverbank. There I saw the attraction—a single canoe being powerfully propelled past Kawem village. If anybody from outside the village used "our" river, it was rare enough to become a public spectacle.

Today the priest from Pirimapuan passed us as he traveled to the Catholic villages east of us. Father Julius sat tall and straight, while the mist flattened his hair and made his black robe cling to his sturdy frame. He stared straight ahead, not even acknowledging our existence. The six men who paddled the canoe stole a glance at the crowd, then turned their attention back to their labor.

I felt a nudge at my shoulder and turned to find Han next to me. "He doesn't like us," Han said, pointing with his chin to the priest. Thinking a moment he added, "He has been around here a long time."

"Do you remember when he first came to this area, Han?"

"Yes, I was still a young, unmarried man. The priest was here before any Protestant missionaries came. He didn't live in Kawem or teach us, but he sprinkled water on our heads and told us we were all members of his church."

I looked at Han in surprise and asked, "Do you mean that Kawem once was a Catholic village?"

"Yes, all the villages were Catholic at that time. That didn't change the way we lived. We still practiced our own customs, and we didn't mind being called Catholic because the priest always gave us gifts when he visited Kawem or we visited him in Pirimapuan.

"When Protestant missionaries came to Pirimapuan, we realized they were different. They seemed to care about us as people, not just names written on paper. We decided to become Protestant and invited Tuan Schmidt to live with us. Oh, you should have seen the priest when he heard about that."

Han's eyes glazed as he described the scene in detail. "Father Julius stood in his canoe and shouted to his paddlers, 'Push this canoe away from Kawem.' He stood and planted his feet apart, while the canoe wobbled. His face twisted with anger, and his blue eyes flashed. He pointed over the crowd gathered on the beach and uttered a curse. 'You have rejected the truth. Now the rivers will rise and rise until they cover your entire village and wash it away. Kawem will be no longer.'"

"Oh Dafit, we were scared," Han admitted. "We didn't know much about white people. We didn't know if he really had the power to drown our village. We weren't true believers yet, so we didn't know how to trust God. I'm not sure why we didn't just return to the priest, but I'm glad now that we didn't."

As I learned more of the history of Irian Jaya and especially the South Coast, I began to understand what had taken place in the early years. Conservative European Catholic churches sent the first missionaries to that area. In its most simple outworking, those priests believed salvation comes from Jesus Christ but is administered only through the Roman Catholic Church. With that philosophy, it was easiest to bring tribal people into the church first, then use that proximity to teach them. Some priests felt competition from other Christian missionaries, whom they considered heretics. In their zeal, they did whatever they could to claim entire villages before the Protestants could get there.

Han told me, "One day the priest walked into the village of Airo and called all the people together who had not yet been baptized. He asked these people to stand with their hands outstretched while he walked past them and sprinkled water on their heads. One of his helpers followed and gave each of the new 'Catholics' a handful of tobacco as payment for participating."

Aha. Some of my scattered thoughts came together and began to make sense. Under the Indonesian system, when the priests baptized people into their church, they "owned" them. The government would not allow Protestants or others to discuss their beliefs with these people. The people were Catholic in name only and still practiced their animistic traditions, but officially no other missionary could teach in those villages except by invitation. As I watched the priest's canoe disappear up the river, I wondered if we would receive any invitations from other villages.

Little did I know how God would accomplish this, but a few days later He began working toward that end.

The screaming began at the far end of Kawem village and worked its way to our house. "He's burned! He'll die!"

Dropping the book I was reading, I ran from our yard in the direction of the screams. I stopped abruptly at the home of Guru Semboor. Semboor was a teacher in the government school at Kawem, but I knew he and his family had left the week before to visit relatives. *Who was in their house*?

I called, then ducked under the low eaves and entered the house. Though the sun shone brightly outside, the house was dark because Semboor had boarded the windows before he left. In the dim light of a kerosene lantern I saw a man stretched out on the floor, surrounded by several men I did not recognize.

"We are from a village on the Julianna River." One Kayagar man became the spokesperson. "This man," pointing to the figure on the floor, "is the teacher in our school. He was lighting a pressure lamp when it exploded in his face. I'm afraid he is dying. Our local medical worker could not help him. We have heard that you help people. Can you do something for him?"

I lifted the lantern and approached the burned figure, then drew back involuntarily. His face and upper body were very badly burned, and the stench overpowered me. "When did this happen?" I asked.

"Two days ago. It took us that long to carry him here in our canoes."

"Oh, God," I whispered in prayer, "what can I do?"

It was dry season, so we couldn't get a floatplane on our river. To bring this man by canoe to a better landing spot would take another day, and he might not survive that long. I began instructing my Kawem friends standing outside.

"Yahya, open the windows."

"Zet, go back to my house and ask Kathy to give you some clean sheets and all of the boiled water we have available."

"Our visitors are tired and hungry. Someone take them to the church and give them food." As people left the small house, I had room to work. I slowly peeled back layers of clothing, old bandages, and leaves which had been used to cover his burns. Then I examined him as best I could and ran back to the radio at my house.

"Senggo, Kawem. We have a medical emergency." Throughout every day mission doctors in Irian Jaya took turns monitoring the single side band radio. I knew from experience that Dr. Ken Dresser at Senggo would be standing by right now.

"Kawem, Senggo. What's up, Dave?" Ken's unruffled voice had a calming effect.

Explaining the situation, I quickly got to my main point. "Is there any way I can evacuate this man to get better treatment?" Then I began answering Ken's questions: "No, the river's too low for a landing. No, there's no one else within a day's journey who can do more for him than I can." With a sinking feeling I anticipated Ken's response.

"You'll have to do the best you can for him there, Dave. He might die under your care, but he will die for sure if you try to send him anywhere else. Now let me give you some instructions." Ken and I conferred, on and off, for the better part of that afternoon as I treated the teacher. It took hours to clean his burns and the infection which had already begun. I cut up several new blankets from the store to make clean bandages. We started boiling extra water on our wood stove. This man's survival became our family and church project for the next few weeks.

He lived. It was a full month before he could come to my house to thank me and say goodbye. As he left, someone asked me in a low voice, "Why did you do so much for him? You know he's a Catholic teacher, don't you? He is one of the most vocal opponents to Protestants working on the Julianna River." If I had been less tired, I would have been angry at this question. As it was, I just answered, "He is a man who needed help. We did what was right. Everything else is between him and God."

We found out later there were others watching, too.

It wasn't long before I noticed a new man in Kawem village. Strangers occasionally passed through our area, but this man stayed. Eventually Haram brought him to meet me. "Dafit, this is Lukat." That was a rather abrupt introduction, but I could see from Haram's face there was more. "Lukat used to live here in Kawem."

That made me curious. The Kayagar didn't move from place to place as individuals. I only knew of a handful of people who had left one village to become part of another. In each of those cases they had committed a cultural sin and were running from punishment. *What caused this man to run from Kawem?* I wondered.

"Remember when a man from Kawem gave his child as a peace payment?" Haram asked me.

"Yes, I do, Haram. He did that to avoid a fight over his debt. You explained how that custom can illustrate what God did in giving His Son as a peace offering between Himself and mankind."

"There is another type of peace offering, Dafit. That's when two families or villages are already fighting and they want to stop. To seal the peace they exchange a child. That child will be raised by the other family as one of their own."

I knew Haram was trying to tell me something more than a cultural lesson, but he was following the Kayagar custom of "beating around the bush." I began asking direct questions in my typical American way. "Haram, you say the child is raised as one of their own. Is the child told about his status? Does he know where he came from? I know clan and village ties are very important to your people. Does this child ever actually become a member of the other village?"

Now Haram was almost laughing (and Lukat looked embarrassed). "No, the child will always identify with his original village. For example, if Kawem fought with the village of Haipu and they wanted peace, they might have exchanged a child some time ago. When that child grew up, he could choose to stay in Haipu or come back to Kawem. If he stayed in Haipu, he might come back to Kawem to visit occasionally."

Haipu was one of three Kayagar villages drawn together into an area known as Haipugir, about a day's journey straight through the rain forest to the east of us. Haram, the Dani evangelists, and I had often wondered how we could reach that area with the gospel, but it was a solidly Catholic area.

Suddenly I knew where Haram was taking me. I looked in amazement at the visitor, Lukat, as Haram chuckled and said, "Lukat was that peace child. When Lukat became an adult, he stayed in Haipu and married. Despite that, he was always considered a member of his birth clan. Lukat remembered living in Kawem with his family, and he remembered the missionary's teaching about salvation through Jesus Christ alone. Over the past months, everyone in Haipugir had heard about the gospel's movement through the villages on the Cook and Kronkel Rivers. Lukat had talked to others in Haipu about true Christianity. Finally the village chief in Haipu said, "Lukat, we have heard enough talk from you. We're interested, but if the priest hears about this he won't be happy. I want you to meet Tuan Dafit in Kawem and tell him my words. We will welcome him if he wants to visit us."

This is what pioneer missionaries dream of—a whole new area open to Christ. Even I, with all my youthful pride, had to admit I didn't know what to do next. Missionary coworker, Don Richardson, lived in Miyaro and was close enough to Haipugir to have semi-regular contact with them. Don received word of this invitation about the same time as Kathy and I did. He graciously became my mentor in this outreach.

Kathy and I flew into the Miyaro airstrip about a month later. Carol Richardson invited Kathy and the girls to stay with her while Don and I trekked from Miyaro to Haipugir. When we arrived at their home, we learned Don and I couldn't go to Haipugir immediately. For some reason the people weren't ready to see us yet, so our family settled in for a week's unplanned, but necessary, vacation. Kathy was glad to visit with another Western woman. I discovered that Don was a very accomplished chess player. I played several games of chess that week and never came close to a win. The worst part came when, after I lost, Don would reset the game board and—from his phenomenal memory—replay the game to show where I went wrong. Ouch!

We also spent time discussing the situation at Haipugir. "Friend Dave," Don said one evening over the chessboard, "have you thought about what you're going to do after our visit to Haipugir? If these Kayagar want to become Protestants, what will you do?"

Suddenly, I realized I'd been thinking so much about the coming week I hadn't really planned beyond it. "When the villages along the Cook River initiated people movements we've seen little opposition. Here on the eastern side of the rain forest I can't supply as much material or spiritual support to the new believers. You've been through this before, Don. What would you suggest?"

"The most important thing to do, Dave, is use whatever opportunity you get to preach and teach the gospel."

"Of course we'll do that, Don, but I get the feeling you have more in mind."

"The people of Haipugir have already done a courageous thing just by inviting you, a Protestant missionary, to visit them in their Catholic village. They'll almost certainly invite you now to send either a Western missionary or national evangelist to live with them." I could see Don was getting excited about this. "Even with that invitation," he continued almost without pause, "you can't assume they fully understand the gospel or have made any real commitment to follow Christ. You have to see this more as an opportunity for continued contact than as a one-time evangelistic thrust.

"When we leave Haipugir in a few days you'll go back to Kawem. You'll be several days' travel from them. In this culture twenty miles is the same as two hundred. 'Out of sight' means 'out of mind,' too. You have to maintain regular contact and regular teaching until you can place a missionary or evangelist here. I suggest you list your resources and make a plan. Can you manage to get someone over there at least once a week to teach God's Word?" Without waiting for my reply, Don went on making plans. "You could alternate with Mbitmber, John Semboor, Lukas Kogoya, and some of your other Dani evangelists. Then you can begin the process of bringing in an evangelist. They have a government school, so you don't have to provide a teacher. Also, we should ask the field leadership about assigning one of the new missionary couples to this area."

"Dave," he almost shouted. "This could be the beginning of a great movement!"

After that, our actual visit to Haipugir was almost anticlimactic. Don and I set out walking the next morning. Around Kawem where most of the land was swampy, we had to rely on river transportation, but this area alternated between swamp and vast sand dunes, interspersed by sluggish rivers. We could walk almost all the way between Miyaro and Haipugir. We left early in the morning so we could arrive there before the stifling one-hundred-degree heat of late afternoon.

To get to the village of Haipu, we had to walk through the two other villages which formed the larger region of Haipugir. We found a curious mixture of responses which ranged from hostility to scrutiny all the way to indifference. The reception we received in Haipu, however, made up for all that. The people, led by their chief and our new friend, Lukat, were waiting on the pathway. As soon as the first person spotted us, a cry went up which passed from one to another, alerting the entire village.

"*Tuan Dafit sudah datang!*" the shouts rang out. "David has come!"

"Welcome to our village," the chief grabbed our hands. Lukat was right behind him to repeat the gesture. I saw relief in their eyes. They had gone out on a limb, defying both the local priest and the other villages in the area, to invite me here. I had come through for them. Once again, I wished I understood more of their culture and thought processes so I could better understand these social forces. As long as God kept control and moved me in the right direction, though, I was content to leave it in His capable hands.

Don and I soon stood in the *Balai Desa* (the village hall). The people had been sitting there waiting for us for hours. This would be our first opportunity to share the gospel with the people of Haipu. I would have been happy to let Don speak first. He knew, though, as well as I did, that I had to take the lead because I would have the continuing responsibility for their spiritual growth. "I am not the first missionary to visit your village," I began, and immediately had all their attention. "This man Lukat was the first one to tell you God's story. That makes him a missionary, too." People looked back and forth at one another, digesting this statement. As they realized what I said, they began smiling at Lukat. "Years ago when most of you were still children, God used Lukat, and the entire village of Haipu, to illustrate His way." I now had everyone's full attention.

"For a long time there were bad feelings between the villages of Haipu and my own village of Kawem. You have heard the stories." Heads nodded. "Each village sent raiding parties against the other. You never knew when it was safe to travel on the rivers or into the forest. Wisely your fathers decided they must make a real peace between the villages." Again people looked toward Lukat, because they already knew the rest of that story. I plunged on.

"The people of Kawem chose a child. They gave that child to this village of Haipu. When you received that child, you agreed to maintain peace between the villages. That peace has lasted until this day because that child is still with you." Now it was my turn to look at Lukat.

"Tuan Dafit," several voices spoke at once, but one carried louder than the rest. "That is our way, but you said it is God's way. What do you mean?"

"You know many of the stories from the Bible." I took the chance that they did know some of the stories basic to all of Christianity and paused to let them respond by nodding their heads. "You know God created the world and the first people within this world. You know those people disobeyed God and would not follow His ways. God used many ways to show these people He loved them, but they were too stubborn and rebellious to follow Him. Some people even worshipped spirits and forces rather than the God who created them. Finally God provided the best way for people to have peace with Him. He gave His Son, His only Son . . ."

"Tuhan Yesus!" the men shouted, anticipating my words. I smiled.

"That's right. God gave His Son, named Yesus, to make peace with man. If any person or village chooses to follow Yesus, they can have peace with God. God will give them the power to become His children." As I continued to explain this path to salvation, I glanced at Don's smile. He had pioneered this "redemptive analogy" among the Sawi years before this. Only in the last year or so had we learned that the Kayagar practiced a similar custom. When Don used this among the Sawi, it led to a large people movement and tremendous church growth. Although the Kayagar did not respond immediately to this analogy, both Don and I could see now how his God-inspired insights would have tremendous impact beyond his own immediate area of ministry.

"God gave this custom to your fathers many years ago. Even though they did not understand the spiritual significance, they used this custom to maintain peace and balance in this world. Now God wants you to see beyond your own practices to understand how much He wants you to have peace with Him."

Don and I stayed in Haipu that night and into the next day. As we left, the chief reminded us of the results of that visit, paralleling Don's insights of a few days before. "Tuan Dafit, we want you to teach us more about God's way. We understand that God wants us to have peace with Him, but we need to hear and understand more. When can you come here again?"

It wasn't long before I did return, this time with Mbitmber. This time the opposition was ready. The local teacher invited Mbitmber, Lukat, me, and the village leaders to his home.

"Here is the book we both use." He held up a Bible. "We pray to the same God, we acknowledge the same Jesus. We have some differences, but are these differences so great that you—" and now he looked at the village leaders "—have to leave our church and start another?"

I was frustrated. He wanted to talk about theology, knowing the Kayagar wouldn't understand our discussion. Every time I tried to answer him simply, he would interrupt and say, "That's not such a great difference that you should disturb our way of life."

Arguing was not the way to go. I needed to reach the hearts of the Kayagar. Turning to the men from Haipu, I began, "Do you men know of the village of Kaipom on the other river?"

"Yes," they said hesitantly.

"Do you remember how the people of Kaipom used to live?"

Some of the men began to answer. Then, realizing that I wasn't expecting a real answer, they looked, first to one another, then to me. "We remember."

"Think about how they live now." I stopped. Their response came in the form of a question.

"Do you mean that your God changes the way people live?" the chief asked.

"Now you understand. Following God is not being Catholic or Protestant—or following a priest or missionary. It is not learning to read the Bible. It is not being baptized. It is not following certain rules either. We Christians just believe God loved us so much he sent His Son to pay for our sins. We trust Him and do whatever He says because we love Him."

The men told the priest, "We have seen the people in Kaipom. We aren't afraid of them anymore. They are different. We think there is a difference between what you teach and what Dafid teaches. We want new hearts like God gave Mbitmber, Lukat, and the people in Kaipom."

CHAPTER TEN APPLICATION GUIDE

"For it is by grace you have been saved, through faith—and this not from yourselves, it is the gift of God—not by works, so that no one can boast" Ephesians 2:8-9 (NIV).

The Kayagar learned an important lesson—it doesn't matter what religion people embrace or what fetish they have, everyone is lost without trusting Christ. Satan has deceived people all over the world with the lies that we must perform certain acts or have the approval of certain people. We all struggle with these false beliefs. Yet, we have salvation through the works of Jesus only, and God approves only the works of His Son. Some people say grace means "God's Riches At Christ's Expense." This is a good definition for the unmerited favor God gives us. God loves us, accepts us, and values us because of His own creative and redemptive works.

What a blessing to know our worth and salvation doesn't depend on things we do or other people do. How our hearts fill with gratitude when we grasp this truth. It changes our whole outlook on life. The pressure is off, and we obey God's commands from love and gratitude, not from fear.

When situations come up, we draw unconsciously on our belief system. Our beliefs spawn thoughts. Our thoughts generate emotions. Our emotions explode into action.

It is hard to change deep beliefs and thought patterns, but Paul shows us the way. "Therefore, I urge you, brothers, in view of God's mercy, to offer your bodies as living sacrifices, holy and pleasing to God—this is your spiritual act of worship. Do not conform any longer to the pattern of this world, but be transformed by the renewing of your mind" Romans 12:1-2 (NIV).

PONDER these Scriptures:

Acts 15:10-11; Romans 3:22-24; Romans 4:2-8.

PRAISE God for grace.

Praise God for His grace (giving us what we don't deserve).

Praise God for His mercy (not giving us what we do deserve).

PEER into your heart.

Are you using the faith God gave you to trust in Jesus Christ alone?

Do you know God loves, values, and accepts you because you are in Christ?

PRAYER

Gracious Father, I praise You for the grace You poured on me though I didn't deserve it. Thank You for being so indescribably caring and kind. I pray for those who don't appreciate Your gifts. Please give them spiritual insight. Help me have an attitude of gratitude. Please help missionaries around the world share the gospel clearly and simply, without passing on cultural baggage. As missionaries share Your truth, I pray people will grasp the gospel and reject false beliefs. In the Name of Jesus I ask these things. Amen.

CHAPTER ELEVEN

God Gives Unity

"Dafid, where are you going with the *balanga* (cooking pot)? What are you cooking?" People in Kawem shot many questions at me as I carried a big, round pot which always reminded me of the large cauldrons seen in fictional illustrations of witches. Curiosity and hubbub grew, and quite a crowd gathered by the time I had collected some pig fat, wood ash, and fire kindling.

"*Yahanap-Yahanap* (friends)," I addressed the group. Then I looked directly at Waipe, once again my friend. "You just finished working for a month to buy your wife a new dress." He smiled proudly.

"Natan, you have new shorts, and you also gave your old shorts to your son. I like the way you tied them up with string until he grows into them."

My eyes moved over the whole group. "Does everyone like wearing new clothes?" Heads nodded and voices hummed in agreement.

"One bad thing about clothes is you have to wash them with soap. Where can you get this soap?" The question hung in the air as they looked at each other.

"From *toko*." Someone finally answered. Everybody laughed.

"Yes, but how did it get made so I could sell it? In my country now people buy soap from *tokos*, too. Many years ago, though, people in my country made their own soap. You would have to work two full days for a large bar of soap." In our *toko* we had to pass along our costs, and the local government fixed the wages we could pay. The cost of necessities seemed unfair to us, but there was little we could do. Making soap instead of buying it was one way I could think of to help.

"What if you didn't have to buy soap? Wouldn't it be better if you could make it yourself?" Without waiting for an answer, I rushed on, "Let me show you how it's done." I had never made soap before, but I had done some research and was ready to give it a try. "We have everything we need right here in Kawem."

The Kayagar seldom used materials from outside the rain forest. The prolific sago trees gave them most of their staples. The pith gave them sago flour, fronds built walls for their houses, leaves covered roofs, and the bark formed flooring. The women wove mats and skirts from grasses. So I thought they would be happy to use fat from their pigs and wood ashes from their fires to make soap.

Standing over a pot, stirring hot goop in the burning sun wasn't my favorite thing to do, but I stayed cheerful while giving my step-by-step explanation of what I was doing. The people watching called to relatives, "Come and see what Dafid is doing." They watched carefully and listened closely to every word I said. Occasionally they offered encouragement such as, "It's wonderful that you can make soap."

Finally, I turned to them with pride and showed them the finished product. "It is a little gooey yet, but it will harden with time." We all smiled, and I was thinking it was worth the effort.

People stared in awe and began complimenting me, "Dafit, that is great! Can you show us that again?" Harem Bohowhi, one of my church leaders who was perhaps the most progressive thinker of all, said, "We watched, and now we understand how you did it. This is a wonderful thing you've done, but we don't do things like that." Then he walked away, followed by all the others. Within minutes I stood alone in the heat, with only tired arms and a big mess to show for all my work.

Change is probably the greatest challenge to working among tribal people. Few people see the need for change until their current circumstances become uncomfortable. Even then, they weigh which is worse—staying as they are or making the effort to change. Tribal people in animistic cultures have an even harder time with change, because they fear it will upset the balance of life.

When change does happen, it often causes disunity, because some people embrace it and others don't. In the Kayagar culture, all major decisions were made by consensus. When an individual or group made a decision against that consensus, it ripped at the very core of their life. Many feared Christianity because they saw it bring changes in core beliefs, relationships, and actions. Some people argue that missionaries should never try to change a culture. However, change was coming to Irian Jaya one way or another. The Indonesian government pressed very strongly to have the people wear clothing. To the government, clothes equaled civilization. Naked tribal people were an embarrassment to the government.

Change, progress, and the sequence of change sometimes had mortal consequence. We saw this in what was then named Frederick Hendrick Island, part of the southeastern coast. The people who lived on the island had a tradition of ritualized orgies. Drawn to this island for profit, outside traders began visiting the island and eventually participated in their sexual orgies. As a result, these traders introduced diseases, including venereal diseases. The people on the island had no immunity to these diseases. When we lived in Irian Jaya, it was possible to fly over the island and see the remains of human habitation, yet not one human remained alive.

Since change comes anyway, it is most beneficial to bring change through people who want to give rather than take. While the government forced changes on the people, most missionaries offered opportunities for change that let the people choose. Effective change happens inside a person and works its way out to behavioral changes. Through faith in Christ, primitive people can make a smoother transition into civilization. Sometimes, however, we missionaries want to make changes before the people are ready.

As I look back and write this, it seems we had a lot of encouragement. Then, it seemed to my Western mind to take longer than I expected.

Most missionaries in Irian Jaya were avid readers. Living in the rain forest with no television, local radio, or other entertainment made reading one of our few forms of relaxation. In addition to some lighter reading, I had brought a seven-volume set of church history—heavy books both in size and content. They had gathered quite a bit of dust by now, but I took volume one to Sentani on a short vacation.

Bill Rosenberger, another missionary who enjoyed history, was based in Sentani. Our conversations had prompted me to dig the book out of a steel storage drum and begin reading.

"What are you reading?" Bill came up behind my chair and peeked over my shoulder. "Oh, pretty deep stuff. How can you read it here with all the interruptions?"

"The interruptions aren't the problem for me. I've just put off getting started," I replied. "Now that I'm into it, I'm being reminded about how God has worked through the centuries. I sense God speaking to me about my Western impatience. I've been trying to force some changes and have been getting disappointed because my unreasonable expectations didn't happen.

"There is truth to the saying, 'Rome wasn't built in a day.' Reading this book has reminded me how long it took for my ancestors to change. Look how long it took God to establish the church in Europe. God worked through committed missionaries for centuries, and I'm expecting to plant the Kayagar church and bring it to maturity in a few years?

"Bill," I concluded, speaking as much to myself as to him. "I need to apply a better sense of perspective to what we're doing in Kawem."

We had missionaries from various countries and cultures working together in Irian Jaya, so we often saw needs for change from different perspectives.

"Kawem, Karubaga." The radio brought John Dekker's unmistakable voice into our house.

"Go ahead, John," replied Kathy into the microphone. Then she called out the window to me, "Dave, John Dekker is calling from Karubaga." John was then serving as the RBMU field chairman. This was most likely a business call. I hurried into the house.

"Good morning, Dave and Kathy. I've been giving some orientation to Miss Helga Stuckenberg, a new missionary joining our RBMU team here in Irian Jaya." Kathy and I looked at each other. We had been asking for more missionary help for months.

As if reading our minds, John continued. "Both our ministries among the Kayagar and Sawi need more help. I've challenged

Helga to consider moving to the south coast. Tomorrow she is flying into Kamur to meet John and Esther Mills. You and the Mills can work out a trip to Kawem as well.

"I'm sure you will all enjoy getting acquainted with Helga. If she feels God calling her to either Kamur or Kawem, I'll ask the rest of the executive committee to confirm that as her assignment."

After spending several days visiting John and Esther in Kamur, Helga traveled a full day by canoe to meet us. The people of Kawem had heard about her visit through the forest hot line. As soon as her canoe came into sight that afternoon, a cry went throughout the village. By the time she approached our yard, people lined the river bank. Nonplussed, Helga stepped from the canoe with a smile. She was about five-feet ten-inches tall and attractive. As she greeted us, it was obvious she had come to Irian Jaya from one of our German mission agencies.

We didn't set out to recruit Helga. Instead, we shared what God had done among the Kayagar and Autohoim. "If God has already done this, Helga, can you picture with us what He will do in the future? We're working with seven churches in seven different villages, among two distinct tribal groups. There are ten national teachers and evangelists and their families who minister with us."

"But," Kathy joined in, "We're only touching about twenty-five percent of the Kayagar speakers in this area. There's so much to do and so much more that can be done."

Two days later, Kathy asked, "Helga, it's time to request your flight back to the coast. When would you like me to make arrangements?"

"If you don't mind," she replied softly, "I would prefer to stay here."

With pleasant shock, we listened to Helga tell how she had caught our vision for the Kayagar, and wanted to minister among them. With joy we radioed John Dekker and gave him the news. Then we got busy planning with our first Western coworker.

With time, we learned, along with her adventurous spirit, Helga had strong opinions. So did I. Because she was from another culture and another mission agency, sometimes we disagreed. There were lessons to learn about cross-cultural unity even among us missionaries. The positive benefits far outweighed any problems along the way, and we provided a model for our new believers.

Unity seemed impossible among the Kayagar. They had fought regularly—that's how all the new villages got started. Battles had taken place across village or tribal lines as long as anyone could remember. Nobody trusted anyone outside of their own group. Yet, God was changing this group of new Christians in Kaipom rapidly.

Shortly after the first group baptism in Kaipom, Nggeri and Mbitmber sent word they were going to baptize a group of believers in Amiyam. "Does anyone want to take me to Amiyam for the baptism?" I asked a group of men when I was visiting Kaipom one day. Since I spent most of my time in Kawem, I thought I'd give some of the people here a chance to make money.

Six new believers responded right away, and a few days later they came to get me. I planned to spend Saturday talking with the candidates and Sunday watching the baptism. When we got to Amiyam, the six paddlers beached the canoe, then one of them carried my small bag to the teacher's home where I was spending the night. I was ready to pay them and say goodbye, when I noticed they were unloading grass mats rolled into bundles and tied with rattan.

"What are you doing?" I asked.

"We're staying for the baptism and then taking you home again."

"Oh, you don't have to do that," I replied. "You can leave now, and I'll get someone else to take me back."

They looked as though I had offended them. "Since we were the first village that had a baptism, we thought we should witness this one. We want to heal bad feelings between the villages, so we can be true brothers in Christ. We learned a hymn to sing for the new believers here."

I wondered if this day were an exception, or possibly the prelude to true cooperation between the new churches. Indonesian tribal people want to belong. The Western idea of a totally independent local church doesn't fit into Indonesian life. Because of this, RBMU, Unevangelized Fields Mission, and Asia Pacific Christian Mission had begun an organization to help the new churches join together in a province-wide fellowship. *Gereja Injili Irian Jaya*

(The Evangelical Churches of Irian Jaya) had started with churches from the Dani tribe and had expanded to include representatives from the Yali, Kimyal, Hupla, and other tribal groups. Now that we had churches organized, I wanted our believers to share in this broader fellowship.

John Mills and I, overseeing the only RBMU ministries on the south coast of Irian Jaya, planned to send representatives from our churches to the next *Gereja Injili Irian Jaya (GIIJ)* annual meeting. I chose Hermanus Kawem and John chose Amhwi, a Sawi church elder, and Yana, one of the Dani evangelists working in Kamur. John and I assumed our churches would join at that meeting. However, Yana, designated as our spokesperson, told the organization they had come only as observers.

John and I felt frustrated. Now it would be another year before we could become members. On the good side, this showed us we had more work to do. If our representatives didn't know why they were there, we had internal communication to handle before we joined a larger group. We used the time to good advantage and were working more in unity the next year.

During that year, we organized two churches—*Klassis Sawi*, for the Sawi people; and *Klassis Kokor* for the Kayagar. *Klassis* meant a regional group of local churches. *Kokor* was a name the church leaders invented to represent the two rivers on which our Kayagar lived. The Cook, which they spelled Kook, and the Kronkel, which they pronounced Koronkel.

Each local church began the process by further organizing their own leadership. They confirmed the elders already in positions of responsibility, and they added new elders since the churches had grown. The leadership then met together to organize the *Klassis*. We set our first "business meeting" for the next month in Kaipom. It would take place over a two-day period.

Helga, Kathy, our daughters, and I took the two-hour canoe journey for these meetings. When we arrived in Kaipom, we found a guest house built just for these two days.

The business meetings went as well as could be expected. This was new to all of us, and I was surprised that our work was done by the second afternoon.

Stepping out of the church building, I noticed unusual activity in the village, but I didn't think much about it. "Kathy," I called "are you and the girls ready to leave? Do you know where Helga is?"

Instead of a reply, Kathy pointed up the river. Following her finger, I saw the river teeming with canoes. "Look," I shouted to no one in particular, "There's Han and his family, and Waipe, and Hainam from Amaru, and Koper and the folks from Amiyam."

I should have expected this! In missionary circles we used to joke about using "any excuse for a party." In tribal cultures, though, it was more a reality than a joke. Most major decisions or rites of passage are a reason to celebrate. Without telling me, the church leaders had organized the first ever *Klassis*-wide potluck dinner, and they had invited believers from all our villages to it.

Oh, the food! We had sago and fried sago grubs, roast pig, a variety of greens from the forest, fruits galore, and so much more. There were things we didn't recognize and didn't want to ask about. Along with the feasting, we enjoyed singing and listening to testimonies. There were no awkward periods of silence like there sometimes are in Western churches during testimony time. The people were eager to tell all the good things God had done for them.

"See the sun go down?" one of the men said. "God has given us another day of life—and what a good day it has been." People lit fires and sat around for hours talking and singing God's praises. I couldn't help thinking about how this differed from the old "singing" we heard when we first moved to Kawem, when the drums played the incessant "tum-ta-tum" and the monotonous voices began their "uuh, ohh, uuh."

Finally, Hermanus Kawem, newly chosen leader of *Klassis Kokor*, stood on the porch of a house and called for everyone's attention, "Friends, brothers, and sisters in Christ. You all know the stories of our past. We have had times of battle and times of peace. The peace never lasted long, because we had nothing in common except the location of our villages."

"Maybe that was why we fought so much. We lived too close," yelled someone from the crowd. This generated good-natured laughter.

"You're right," chuckled Hermanus. Then he paused and grew very serious. "That is all past. Tonight, around the fires of Kaipom, I hear four different languages. Pointing to Helga and Kathy with his chin, he continued, "we even have people from other countries. From where I stand, I can count people from seven villages. I can't even count how many clans and families are here—Kawem . . . Bohowhi . . . Hahare," as he said each clan name, people from that clan nodded their heads.

"We have always had these differences, and we always will. But now we have something much stronger which draws us together. We are all following Jesus. We all belong to God. For the first time, but forevermore, we are one in Christ!"

CHAPTER ELEVEN APPLICATION GUIDE

"Just as each of us has one body with many members, and these members do not all have the same function, so in Christ we who are many form one body, and each member belongs to all the others" Romans 12:4-5 (NIV).

When your physical body doesn't work in unity, there is a problem. Perhaps you have a growth, injury, or disease that interferes. The same holds true for the spiritual body of Christ. Unity in Christ can cross cultural, racial, economic, social, and generational borders. But injuries and sin can interfere with the unity God wants us to enjoy as Christians.

The key that unlocks the door to unity is found in Philippians 2:1-8. Here is a very loose paraphrase: If you are united with Christ, and this encourages you, then be united with fellow Christians. Don't be vain or selfish, but consider the needs of others as more important than your own. That is the example Jesus set for us. He laid aside all the glory He had with the Father, came to earth, and died a painful and embarrassing death. Our needs were that important to Him.

Just before Jesus gave His life, He prayed for us to live in unity. "My prayer is not for them alone [His twelve disciples], I pray also for those who will believe in me through their message, that all of them may be one, Father, just as you are in me and I am in you..." John 17:20-21 (NIV).

Dave saw God working in hearts, drawing people to unity in Christ. God wants unity among Christians around the world. If our hearts are in tune with Him, we will soon find more harmony in our relationships with others.

PONDER these Scriptures:

Romans 15:5-6; I Corinthians 12:12-27; Ephesians 4:1-6.

PRAISE God for giving us unity in Christ.

Praise Jesus for His example to us.

Praise God through living in unity with other Christians.

PEER into your heart.

How much do I really care about the needs of others?

Am I doing my best to live in unity—forgiving and serving humbly as Jesus did?

PRAYER

Father, Son, and Holy Spirit, I praise You for the unity You display. Thank You for Your love and concern. Bring me into alignment with Your truth. Please remind me when I want my own way. I pray that missionaries will remember they have a common purpose. In the Christian community, let unbelievers see love and unity that will bring glory to Your Name. Amen.

CHAPTER TWELVE

God Gives Wisdom

"Do you see this wound?" said Han, touching a three-inch jagged line. Scars covered his bare chest, proving what a valiant warrior he had been.

I looked closely at the scar he pointed out and exclaimed, "That is very near your heart."

"Yes. I killed three people in that battle, and someone nearly killed me that day, too."

I gazed at Han's face with both horror and fascination. Han sat before me cross-legged, a short, muscular man. In the bright sunshine, it looked as if someone had laid thin spirals of shiny, white wire on his head. He was the leader of the Hahare clan, and I knew he had earned his leadership role by performing fearless deeds. Han's voice boomed as he described the events of that terrible day. He stood and acted out the story—how he had crept toward the village and screamed to scare his enemies. He pulled back an imaginary bow and shot the arrow it held, then he fell backward, reliving how the arrow someone else shot burned its way deep into his chest. Then he stopped, sat down, took a deep breath, and said nostalgically, "We don't do that anymore. We're Christians now."

Responding to my questioning glance, he continued, "Dafid, there are times I remember the old days when people looked up to me as a courageous hero. That gave me pleasure. Then I think about my life now. God has given me new pleasures. He has forgiven me of many sins, even of leading my clan into battle and killing other people. Now I've been able to lead my family to

Jesus. I've seen my sisters marry and bring their husbands to Jesus. I've seen my son marry into another family and bring that family to Jesus."

I appreciated his honesty; many Kayagar said what they thought I wanted to hear. "Han, I like to hear your stories; they help me understand the Kayagar people. I'm glad, though, that you quit fighting. I'm glad God spared your life because I like you being here with me. Your friendship is God's gift to me. Change has come to the Kayagar—and to all of Irian Jaya. You are still respected as head of your clan, and you are leading them in a spiritual battle now."

He smiled and batted my head affectionately, just as he would have done to his son. Then Han's eyes fixed over my left shoulder. "Dafid, do you want to meet someone who was even worse than I was during those days before we knew Christ?" he asked somewhat mischievously.

My spine tingled as Han eyes stared directly behind me. *Dare I turn and see a person who did worse than he had just described to me? Do I want to know who he is?* I stood quietly, looking at Han as he continued, "This man killed even women and children who got in his way. Everyone was afraid of him."

"Is he close?" I probed.

"Yes, he is close, Dafid." He murmured, "Turn and look."

I summoned my courage and turned slowly. The only man I saw was Aupm, a meek Christian man I saw every day. He smiled as he always did. "Where is this person?" I asked.

Han snickered. "It is Aupm."

Evidently, Aupm had heard some of Han's comments. He nodded his head. "Aupm, you surprised me," I said. He didn't answer.

Han's voice came from behind me. "No, Dafid, Aupm didn't surprise you—God did. You told us when a man follows Christ, he becomes a new person. Why are you surprised that God's Word came true?"

He's paraphrasing II Corinthians 5:17, I thought. "Therefore if any man be in Christ, he is a new creature: old things are passed away; behold, all things are become new." Yes, God was doing new things among the Kayagar people. Things I had hoped for, yet wondered if I would ever see. God was recreating them in His own image. This was happening in the Autohoim tribe, too.

"*Konahare,* Dafid." *Konahare,* meaning hello and goodbye, was the all-purpose Autohoim greeting. Esime waved from across Kaipom village.

"*Konahareo,* Esime." I returned his greeting and kept walking.

A minute later, I heard footsteps and Esime was at my side. "Dafid, how can I talk to God?" he asked.

"What do you mean, Esime? You talk to God all the time. I've heard you pray often."

"No. I'm not talking about praying. How do I talk to God? Like this morning when I saw you; I said *Konahare* and you answered *Konahareo*. Do I say *Konahare* to God when I greet Him?"

Now I understood. He wasn't satisfied just to pray words he heard others pray. He was learning how to develop a personal relationship with God and still show the proper respect. I knew I couldn't answer his questions, I had to help him think through this issue. "When you greeted me this morning, what did you say?"

"*Konahare,*" he answered.

"And what is our relationship?"

"You are my friend, Dafid."

"You love your mother. When you see her, what do you say?"

"*Konahare,*" he repeated.

"You trust and follow the village chief..."

"And I say *Konahare* to him." Esime took over from there. "I see now! I greet my friends, family, and leaders by saying *Konahare*. God is my friend, my family, my leader, and more. I think I can say *Konahare* to Him. What do you think, Dafid?"

"I think you've answered your own question, Esime," I said, patting his arm.

My thoughts drifted back to the United States just before we left for Irian Jaya. We were at Kathy's parents' house, and Gwen was learning to climb. She climbed up my leg and into my lap. She didn't stop there, however, she climbed on the back of the sofa, and was beginning to climb the wall, reaching toward a picture. I said, "Stop that," swatted her bottom lightly, and put her back on my lap to keep her safe.

"This is normal," my father-in-law said. "Gwen is doing what all kids do. Once they start exploring, you can't stop them—all you can do is guide and direct."

This good advice came in handy now that our new babes in Christ were beginning to explore. They didn't need restriction or control—they needed guidance and direction. Spiritual exploration is good; but without guidance, it can lead to heresy.

As the churches grew and we trained new leadership, I tried to meet with these men as often as possible. Obviously, I met more often with leaders in Kawem and Amaru because they lived closer to me. The evangelists who lived in Kaipom and Amiyam trained the leaders in these more distant villages. I enjoyed a daily meeting with the elders in Kawem. They came to my home for Bible study and prayer, although it was different from a Western Bible study. The Kayagar struggled with Bible study due to their concept of time. They had no written, or even much oral, history. They couldn't picture a sequence of years and apply it to themselves.

Their culture didn't teach them to question and reason either. Older people taught younger people, "This is how it is done." And the younger people accepted that. I didn't want them to learn God's Word by rote, and I was encouraging questions.

We had been reading about how God planted a new church in Asia Minor. When we came to Acts 12:23, we read about Herod's death. Tadeus interrupted, "I don't understand something."

"What do you mean, Tadeus?" I asked.

"This man Herod is a king. I remember reading about Joseph and Mary running away from King Herod when Jesus was a baby, but is King Herod still alive in this passage? This would be a very long time. Were these two different men with the same name?"

Once again, God surprised me. Tadeus had lived his whole life in a culture that didn't think about time. Now he had compared Scripture to Scripture, then measured it against his lifetime. He had concluded, with no help from me, there were two different King Herods—and he was right. He had taught his people a new concept. My heart smiled the way a father's heart in the States smiles when his son graduates from high school.

Our people were growing up spiritually, and we saw them maturing in other areas of their lives as well.

Helga had been living in a small building until we built a house for her. Her new house was the first wooden one in the area. A missionary carpenter was coming to oversee the construction, and we wondered if we could get enough lumber. Some men from Kaipom came to us and said, "If you will buy two long saws, we will saw lumber for Helga's house." Mbitmber had seen Indonesian workmen using a pit saw, so he told them he would help build a big frame. They would roll the large logs on top of this frame. One man would stand on top of the frame while another man stood underneath, and they could use a two-handled saw about four-feet long. The saws cost only about twenty-five dollars each, and I thought it would be a good investment. If they sawed the lumber, great. If they didn't, I still had the saws.

They used a wood similar to cypress. The first boards they sawed were atrocious, but they improved with practice. After a few tries, I told them I would buy the lumber they had sawed. They brought the lumber to Kawem by canoe, and I paid them the wage the government had set. The people were thrilled! They bought out the *toko*.

Before they left, Esime came to me and said, "We've had a great time. Look at all the presents we bought for our families. But if you keep paying us, we'll spend it on things we don't need. We talked it over and decided we want you to mark down what we earn. When we have enough saved, will you buy aluminum roofing for us? We'll build a new church and put the aluminum on the roof."

I could hardly contain my excitement. No other church on the south coast had built their own church and put an aluminum roof on it with their own resources. This was their idea, and they trusted me to hold the money they earned. We built a nice house for Helga, and the men from Kaipom made enough money to build their church. What a blessing for everyone. Today we would call this a win-win situation.

When they had saved enough, I ordered the aluminum. I stored it in the *gudang* (store house). The next time they came with wood, I took them to the *gudang* and opened the door. "There it is. It's all yours," I said. I showed them they had enough for the church roof and I showed them how I had kept track in the book. They looked at it, they looked at each other, and they looked at me. "You mean it, don't you? It's really ours."

After they finished sawing lumber to earn the aluminum, they continued sawing lumber to build their wooden church. They even made benches inside. I gave them a keg of nails just so I could have a part in it, but they did it all. They had seen a church building with an aluminum roof, but they had never seen a church building made from lumber. This was their offering to God in response to all He had given them.

God not only helped the Autohoim construct a strong building, He helped both the Autohoim and Kayagar establish a strong leadership structure for their church, too. The church in Kawem had chosen Daniel as an elder, primarily because he was a leader in the Kawem clan. I had high hopes for him. Yet, as time progressed, Daniel didn't come to our meetings. He always had something more important to do. A year passed, and it was time to choose elders again. "Brothers and sisters," I began, "I don't know what to do. I want you to make decisions for your church. I don't want to tell you what to do, but I have a responsibility as the one who led you to Christ and as a member of this church. Daniel is a fine man, a true believer, and very smart. I'm not sure he should be an elder though. He hasn't attended our Bible studies and prayer times..."

Han knew what to do. He spoke up, "I have been thinking this, too. Daniel is a fine man, but he is still young. How can we have a leader who doesn't study the Bible with us? How can we have an elder who has more important things to do than pray for his people?" Facing Daniel, he continued, "Daniel, you are a good man. You have grown up among us, and we have seen your faith. God doesn't mean for every Christian to serve as a leader in His church. Look at me," Han continued, tapping his chest. "I have been a clan leader. I have proven my bravery. I am wise and respected, yet I've never been a church elder. I am content to do whatever God wants me to do. You are a family leader. Be content to work for God wherever He puts you, and don't seek a position you cannot fulfill properly."

Four other members stood in succession and confirmed Han's words. They had resolved a conflict in love. They had averted a crisis. As I left that meeting, I wondered how much longer they would need me.

In the early days of our people movement, we had begun a Bible school for the new leaders. The men from several villages came together at Kawem one week a month for studies. They applied their knowledge in their villages the rest of the month. After three years, I began to teach them public speaking. As a final assignment, I asked each man to prepare a short Bible message and deliver it to the rest of the group. I thought I would hear my own sermons repeated in their language. Instead, the men expounded on common Bible passages with intelligence and understanding.

It was Esime's turn to give the message. We sat cross-legged on the floor of our little schoolroom waiting to hear what he would share. "Use your Bibles and find what Paul wrote to us in I Timothy chapter five. We will read verses one and two."

I almost fell backward on the floor. We had never studied I Timothy together. It was apparent He had been studying alone with God.

While the men were finding the verses in their Bibles, Esime said, "Here Paul is teaching how Christians should treat each other." Looking briefly at me, Esime went on, "There are things in our culture Dafid doesn't know. There are things we have not told him because we are embarrassed. Now that we are Christians, we know these things do not please Jesus." Esime had my full attention as he focused on the final sentence in this passage, "...treat younger women as sisters, with absolute purity."

His eyes swept the group of men. Some of them looked at the floor. "When we became young men and began having the feelings men have, our fathers taught us to have relations with as many girls as possible, but not to let the girls' fathers catch us."

Several men stole glances at me. Esime didn't stop. "You know our fathers told us not to have relations with our own sisters. It is taboo to even think of such a thing. Here Paul says to treat all women as sisters and think pure thoughts about them. We need to do this. Our fathers also taught us to protect our sisters. Now God tells us to protect all women."

The men nodded their heads. It was settled. His teaching totally changed one aspect of their culture in one short message.

After class, I stumbled to our house in a daze. "Kathy, you'll never guess what happened now." I told her about Esime's message and the way the other men responded. I ended with, "I just don't understand how he knew all of that."

Kathy grinned and shrugged. "It just proves that the Holy Spirit is a better teacher than you are, Dave."

God showed me one more time how much the Holy Spirit was teaching His people. It was exactly one week before we left Kawem for a new ministry in the Irian Jaya highlands. We were attending the third united *Klassis* meeting, which was held in Amaru that year. We sat on bark-covered wooden benches in the church building. There were seven villages represented that year. Six had organized churches now, and one was beginning to organize. The Dani evangelists and representatives from nearby Sawi churches also attended. Everyone wore their best—shirts, long pants, and even sandals.

Babak Camat gave a speech, which officially opened the meeting. *Babak* was a term of respect like father or mister, and *Camat* was the title of this local government official. He was an appointed official and a Muslim.

Business meetings are necessary, even if we don't look forward to them. The Indonesian custom was to walk to the front of the building, stand straight, and read a written report very formally. Originality was not highly valued, so the reports all sounded similar—telling the number of buildings, number of people baptized that year, etc.

Through the meeting, I relived our years working with the Kayagar and Autohoim. I heard, "We have one church building, one school building, our evangelist has a house, and our school teacher has a house." Then off my mind wandered, remembering when Mbitmber came as the evangelist to Kaipom.

I heard, "This year we built seventeen pews." I wondered, *Is God bored at business meetings, too?*

Lastly, Esime, now an elder in the Kaipom church, went to the front. He was wearing shorts and he didn't have a written report in his hand. Everyone stared. Esime looked over the crowd and said, "There are still six adults in our village who have not personally committed themselves to Jesus Christ. Would you pray that they will believe this year?" He sat down.

Tears welled up in my eyes. I fought to control myself, but then the tears spilled over and I sobbed out loud. My spiritual children had matured, and I would not be "fathering" them anymore. This man understood the core of Christianity; he knew how to prioritize. God had raised up mature leaders who would continue bringing people into a personal relationship with Jesus Christ. This was God's work. It would last forever!

CHAPTER TWELVE APPLICATION GUIDE

"If you want to know what God wants you to do, ask Him. He will gladly tell you, for He is always ready to give a bountiful supply of wisdom to all who ask Him. He will not resent it" James 1:5 (TLNT).

All through this book, we've seen God give wisdom to Dave and Kathy. Now we see God giving His wisdom to new believers. Wisdom goes beyond learning. We can buy education, but wisdom is a gift from God. Wisdom tells us how to apply knowledge.

There is great responsibility in learning God's Word. If we know what He wants us to do, and we don't do it—that is sin. Esime was wise. He gained knowledge through reading God's Word, then he applied it and even taught others.

"The fear of the Lord is the beginning of wisdom; all who follow his precepts have good understanding. To him belongs eternal praise" Psalm 111:10 (NIV).

We have all seen people who had a lot of knowledge but didn't apply it. They may be great in their own eyes, but God specializes in giving simple people wisdom and blessing them through it. In God's eyes, human wisdom is nothing. "For the foolishness of God is wiser than man's wisdom, and the weakness of God is stronger than man's strength" I Corinthians 1:25 (NIV).

Open God's book of wisdom (the Bible), and apply its truths. God will inundate you with gifts—peace, love, support, vision, purpose, joy, faith, life, light, grace, unity, and victory.

PONDER these Scriptures:

Proverbs 4:5-11; Colossians 1:28-29; 2:2-3

PRAISE God for His wisdom

Praise God for having wisdom that is _____ (fill in blanks from James 3:17).

Read Romans 11:33-36 aloud in praise to God.

PEER into your heart.

Do you believe God can provide wisdom when you need it?

Do you lean on human understanding or God's wisdom?

PRAYER

All knowing Father, I praise You for Your wisdom, peace, love, and generosity. Thank You for being willing to share Your resources. I pray for those who are needy and don't realize You are there to provide. Please help me remember You are with me always, and You can provide all I need. Please help me share that good news with others. I pray for ____________ (someone you know who has a need). In Jesus' Name, Amen.

CHAPTER THIRTEEN

God Gives Victory

"We just can't spend enough individual time with each person, and it's hard for people who can't read God's Word to learn about Him alone." Kathy sank into a chair and put her head on the kitchen table. "I wish we could clone ourselves and repeat the gospel over and over to people."

I sat next to her and reached over to pat her hand. "Maybe we can't duplicate ourselves, but we could duplicate our words. Mary Widbin has been building up a ministry she calls Regions Cassettes. Other missionaries are making tapes in tribal languages and sending them to Mary for copies. She's also duplicating teaching tapes in Indonesian. I even heard that Stan and Pat Dale's son, Wesley, is coming to Irian to head up that outreach. What do you think of us getting involved?"

We and several other missionaries took advantage of this technology, and soon making and duplicating tapes became a ministry in itself. A few months later we heard two taping experts were coming to visit us.

"Who are these people and how are they going to help us?" Kathy looked up from the banana fritters she was battering.

"Max Winch told me their names are Noela Elvery and Marilyn Malmstrom They worked for Gospel Recordings quite a while. I think they'll make the recordings and we'll duplicate them, but I'm not sure."

It turned out that the home office in Philadelphia thought this ministry had a lot of potential we weren't tapping. Noela and

Marilyn had left Gospel Recordings and were working on their own, helping missionaries improve their communications skills and techniques. These two experts came and showed us how to revamp the entire taping process and make it a powerful tool. Of course, that meant more personnel and an administrator to oversee the whole operation.

Wes Dale did come from Australia to oversee this ministry; but because it was a new organization, his job description changed between the time he applied to the mission and actually arrived on the field. Once he got there, it was evident he wasn't going to fit in the newly defined role. It wasn't long before someone suggested Kathy and I would fit that ministry role. As we prepared for our first furlough, we and our supervisors decided we would begin the taping ministry when we returned from our year in the United States. Our supervisors asked a new missionary couple to replace us so the Kayagar work would continue.

When we got back to the States, however, we heard that the new couple had been called back to Canada by their home office. The man had preached doctrine that didn't agree with his mission agency. When the agency found out what he had taught in several churches, they dismissed him.

Kathy and I looked at that situation and decided if there was no one to take our place, we should go back to Kawem. That was a mistake. I realize now that I was taking responsibilities that belonged to the Lord. It was His work, not ours. We spent one year back in Kawem after furlough. It was a hard year, and we soon realized we were out of God's will for our lives. God also revealed this to our field leaders, and they moved us to Karubaga in the highlands. There we worked in the tape ministry and administration. We felt sure God was closing a chapter in our lives. We moved to Karubaga with peaceful hearts.

Now we see that God used us because we were right for getting the ministry in Kawem started, but we weren't the best people for keeping the work going. I didn't have a lot of skill with coworkers. I had to work with many people in this new position, and the Lord used this time to help me grow in many areas.

We had a large house that had been built specifically for a missionary family who had since left the field. We could house our family as well as the tape ministry. Half of the upstairs was our taping office. Because our station housed a hydroelectric system, we also had twenty-four-hour electricity for the first time in many years. That was a blessing, but it also led to a personal problem for me.

Western music is popular around the world. In Indonesia, tapes are available for very little cost. On our shopping trips to town, I often bought several new tapes with the latest in American popular music. I enjoy having music playing in the background as I work, so this became a habit. One day I realized most of the tapes included songs about drinking, adultery, divorce, loss of work, and other negative situations. During this time, I was struggling to keep a consistent quiet time with the Lord. Every time I got on track, something would get me sidetracked again. God spoke to me about these two things in His quiet way, but I rationalized my actions and procrastinated about doing anything to correct the situation.

We had ten to fifteen missionaries living at Karubaga, plus frequent visitors. On Sunday mornings we each went to local Dani or Indonesian churches. On Sunday nights we gathered in one of the missionary's homes, and listened to a taped church service from the States. One night we gathered in the home of Gail Berryman, an Australian missionary. I sat in a wooden rocking chair in the corner of her living room. As we sang "Amazing Grace," I felt as though the room fogged over and I heard God talking in an almost audible voice. I looked around startled, but no one else seemed to notice.

"Dave, you've been bothered by the lack of time we are spending together and the time you spend listening to things of this world. When are you going to do something about it?"

For the rest of that night, I was tuned out of the service. It was as if the Lord and I talked business alone in that corner. It was a time of conviction, confession, forgiveness, and recommitment. I planned what actions I would take as a result of my decision.

When we went home, I went upstairs and put every secular music tape in a closet. Eventually, I erased the cassettes and taped over them. Since most of the mission station and surrounding villages didn't start moving until about 7:00 A.M., I got up at 6:00 the next morning for a quiet time of study and prayer. I went to my office alone and spent one-half hour with the Lord. I enjoyed it so much, the next week I got up at 5:30. I started by walking a mile and talking aloud to God. It was dark at that hour, but I eventually learned the path so well that I rarely used the flashlight I brought. Then I went to my office for the half-hour time I'd established the week before. The next week I thought, *I can get up earlier than this.* So I started getting up at 5:00 and spending ninety minutes with God. I'd put a pot of water on our electric hot plate and go for my walk. By the time I returned, the water was boiling and I made a large mug of tea, sweetened with wild honey. I carried the tea to my desk and spent the next hour in Bible reading, studying, memorizing, and devotional reading. This started an upswing in my life, but it was just a start.

For five years before that, I had tried to memorize Scripture off and on; and I had started memorizing I Peter several times. One of my goals during this renewal time was to stick with I Peter until I memorized it. I learned the first chapter easily. Of course, I had worked on that part several times. When I came to the beginning of chapter two, I had a problem memorizing verse one. "Therefore, lay aside all malice, and all guile, and hypocrisies, and envies, and all evil speaking..." Normally, memorization wasn't too difficult, and I didn't understand why this part was so hard. Then, one morning in my quiet time God showed me I was having problems putting this Scripture into action. I realized I had envy for some of my missionary colleagues. They were doing things I wished I could do, but couldn't, either because of time pressure, talent, or difference in spiritual gifts. Later I learned some of them envied me for the same reasons.

I faced a hard awakening. I saw that some of the problems I'd had with other missionaries were my fault instead of theirs as I had thought. When I confessed my sin and submitted to the Lord, I had no more trouble memorizing the rest of I Peter. I even memorized II Peter before we left Karubaga. I look forward to seeing Peter one day and telling him about this experience.

I realized I needed to make some things right with other people. I needed forgiveness for things I had thought, said, and done. The next time our field conference came around I asked for five minutes at the end of a business session. My heart beat hard and a hot flush crept over me as I climbed the steps to the platform. It was dead silent. This wasn't on the agenda. Nobody knew what I was going to say, even Kathy. I could still change my mind, but I knew what I had to do.

"I have sinned against many of you specifically and all of you in general." *Well, that was one way to start, and it did get everyone's attention.* "Most of you would never have noticed, but I have had some thoughts against you that were not pleasing to Christ. These thoughts never worked their way into action, but I know they affected my attitude. I was wrong. I am standing here tonight to confess this and ask you to please forgive me."

When I finished, our field director, Frank Clarke, came up the steps as I was going down them. He stopped by me and said, "We do." I just looked at him. Again he said, "We do. We forgive you."

I hadn't thought of response. I only needed to get it off my chest. I was drained of physical strength and emotion by then, but that was the pinnacle of the evening for me. They had forgiven me! God gave me victory, and a weight rolled off me. I could forget the past and go on with my spiritual journey.

If that series of events hadn't happened, I couldn't be doing the job I am doing now. I couldn't have told this story, nor could I have mentored others. This event tore down the barriers between God and me. It also tore down the barriers between other people and me.

Before this I resented British coworker John Wilson. John had never done anything to cause these feelings; I doubt he even knew about them. John and Gloria worked among the Yali tribe about fifty air miles from us. Now I felt I had to get to know John better. I didn't tell him what was going on in my life; I only wrote and told him I had pledged to pray for him and his ministry for one year. John sent back his schedule for translating the book of Matthew into the Yali language and Gloria's schedule for literacy classes. At the end of the year, he told me unexplained things happened that year. My prayers had made a difference in his life—and in mine. All the barriers were gone, and I realized how much I had lost during those years when I distanced myself from John.

God also used this to teach me that I could participate in a ministry without being physically present. This lesson was essential and caused a major turning point in my life. I couldn't be doing my present ministry without believing this. God gave me opportunities to introduce this idea to others, and many have told me the blessings their prayer ministry has brought them.

As this all took place, Kathy and I had our best year ever. Our field leadership saw a "new me" during our last year in Irian Jaya. We touched lives in a new way and God blessed us mightily.

Dave Martin served as field chairman through most of our time in Irian. Now he had moved to the Philippines and was in charge of all RBMU work in Asia. This year he was back to visit us all at field conference, and he found an excuse to pull Kathy and me aside. "Kathy and Dave, you know the U.S. Board is looking for someone to take charge of the personnel and recruitment work in the home office. Your names have come up..."

"No!" We didn't give Dave the chance to finish his sentence. "We have no immediate plans to leave Irian." We didn't say, "Thanks for thinking of us" or even the spiritually correct, "We'll pray about it."

During our days in RBMU's candidate school, way back in 1972, I had a strange feeling that we would eventually be part of the home office team. That didn't come to my mind now.

By this time our cassette ministry, renamed *Suara Kaset Kristen*, (The Voice of Christian Cassettes), was hitting its stride. We were expanding into new areas of writing and producing programs, rather than just duplicating tapes.

Lukas Kogoya, who worked with us as an evangelist among the Kayagar, was from a Dani village near Karubaga. Shortly after we moved to Karubaga, Lukas and his wife, Rut, took a year off for Bible college. After graduation, Lukas and his family flew into Karubaga for what I assumed was a short break before returning to Kawem. I met them at the airstrip and began the five-minute Dani greeting of ritualized embrace. "I'm so glad to see you two. And look at your children, Sem and Deborah. They are getting so big." We were both weeping freely, which was not part of the ritual. Lukas was my best friend in all of Irian Jaya.

"How long can you stay before you go back to Kawem?" I asked.

Lukas looked at his feet and said, "We're not returning to Kawem."

I was quiet.

He hurried on, "while Rut and I were at Bible college, we both felt God moving us to come here and work with you. Is there any way you can use us?"

God was at work again! We were just putting into place a five-year plan to nationalize *Suara Kaset.* This plan was based on training a national to replace me, but we hadn't come up with a suitable candidate. Lukas was a spiritual and intelligent man who could see a problem and think his way through to solving it. Rut was every bit his equal intellectually, a rarity in a land where marriages were most often arranged by families. Lukas was the only national with whom I could enjoy deep theological discussions in a language foreign to both of us—Indonesian. To think that Lukas might eventually replace me in *Suara Kaset* was a blessing I couldn't have anticipated. Kathy and I looked forward to spending a few years training Lukas and Rut.

In the fall of 1983, we were visiting the girls at school and we went into the Inter-Mission business office in Jayapura. While we were withdrawing cash from our account, a lady handed us a cablegram from my sister, Taffy. "MOM HAS CANCER STOP 3 MONTHS TO LIVE STOP COME QUICKLY"

Stunned, I immediately phoned Taffy's home in the States despite the twelve-hour time difference. I reached a baby sitter who didn't have much information, but I made an appointment to call back. When I called the next day, I learned that my mother had advanced liver cancer; there was no hope for recovery. She was going to live with my brother, Brett, in California. The family thought she would get the best care there.

How could we go home now? Would I ever see my mother again? Our furlough was due to start in six months, but that would be too late according to the doctor's prediction. We had planned to leave when the school year ended and stay in the States for eighteen months, during which time I would finish a master's degree I had been working on by extension. Then we planned to concentrate on deputation. Since we only could leave Irian Jaya for one year without renewed paperwork, I planned to return during our furlough year to renew our visas. During our absence, Lukas would run *Suara Kaset Kristen* with supervision from other missionaries.

We couldn't make a quick decision. After a few days, I went into the mountains around Karubaga. I took only a Bible, songbook, notebook, pen, and bottle of water. As I walked and prayed, I pictured Mom as I last saw her, crying as she said goodbye to our family for four years.

"Don't mind me," she always put herself last. "I'm just being silly. You're doing the right thing, my David." *Was my name the last word I'd ever hear her say?*

It was almost funny how she sensed we were doing God's will, but she wouldn't acknowledge Christ in her own life. She knew the changes she had seen in all of us kids were God's doing. She even knew God was waiting for her to relinquish control of her life and give herself to Him, but she just wouldn't do it.

I wandered higher up the mountain, talking aloud with the Lord. I received curious looks from a few Dani villagers, but by now most knew me as "the man who talked out loud to God." It had become a public joke as I often called to people, "*An kumili-kumili mendek.* (Don't mind me, I'm crazy.) I walked for hours, alternately praying and singing, stopping only to read from the Bible and make some notes on my thoughts. It wasn't as if my will was struggling with God. I didn't have a will in this. I wanted direction. I was ready to do whatever God wanted, but what was that? "Tell me, Lord," I pleaded, my hands stretched toward heaven. Repeatedly, I asked what He wanted me to do. At last I received an answer. "Wait."

Waiting is hard. That is not the answer I wanted to hear, but at least I had an answer. We would continue with our work and not return to the States. As far as I knew, Mom was not a believer. That made the situation extra hard, and we couldn't talk with her about it. I remember several times leaving the house and running somewhere isolated so I could cry alone. During the months that followed, Mom hung on to life. One of my sisters wrote that Mom might have become a Christian. I longed for more assurance than this. We all knew she would often do or say things just to make others happy. I wanted to hear from her own mouth that I would see her again in heaven.

The Indonesian government complicated matters even further when they decided to change procedures for renewing work visas. Up to this point, the cabinet-level Department of Religion had approved missionary visas. Now all foreign workers would come under the authority of the Department of Labor. All changes seem to cause delays. Our visa renewal was in process and had to be complete before we could get an exit and reentry permit. We hoped we wouldn't be delayed. John and Gloria Wilson were leaving about the same time, and we were looking forward to traveling part of the way together. We packed everything and went to our girls' school early so we could participate in the end of school events. The Wilsons got their paperwork and left. We didn't get ours, and we waited. Finally, we decided to go back to the house in Karubaga, unpack, and get back to work while we waited.

Still in Sentani, I rode my bicycle to the field director's office to tell him our decision. As I was ready to leave, Frank Clarke said, "You know, Dave, there is a chance you could leave for furlough right now."

My hand still on Frank's door handle, I asked, "What do you mean?"

"These new regulations seem inconvenient, but there could be a bright side. All of the mission leaders met last week with the local head of the Department of Labor. He said under the new regulations, the government intends to grant more new missionary visas, especially for ministries which have a plan for nationalization already in progress.

"Dave, this means you could give up your current visa, leave the country with an exit-only permit, and then re-apply for a new visa." I could hardly believe my ears. With all the possibilities Kathy and I had thought of, this one never entered our minds.

"What should I do, Frank? The last instructions I had from God were to wait. I'm not going to make this decision myself. I give it to you and the mission leadership. Kathy and I will abide by your decision."

As soon as I left Frank's office, I met Bert Koiriwa, our church president. Bert agreed that he had heard the same news as Frank had. He suggested the same solution.

Frank conferred with the rest of the RBMU executive staff over the short wave radio. They agreed that, given our circumstances, the best thing was to leave with an exit-only permit and apply for a new visa as soon as we got back to the States.

When we left on June 7, 1984, it was Kristen's birthday and we joked that we were giving her an airplane for her birthday. We didn't realize it would be the last time we would be in Irian Jaya as a family.

We chose to go through San Francisco and my brother, Brett, picked us up at the airport and drove us to the house where he lived with his wife, Flora. He even took time off work to shuttle us back and forth to the hospital where Mom hung on to life. Mom wouldn't let us in her room until Brett helped her put on her wig. Chemotherapy had robbed her of her hair.

I had never been this near death in such a sterile environment. In Irian Jaya we had seen people breathe their last breath, but this was different. I was experiencing reverse culture shock and the hospital sounds and smells took me completely out of my element. Orderlies pushed patients on carts through the halls. Small groups of people stood in hallways and waiting rooms talking quietly among themselves. *Are they losing a parent or loved one, too?* I wondered.

Then Brett stood at my side and motioned me through the door of Mom's room. As the door closed behind me, I realized he had not entered with me.

"Oh Mom!" There was so much I had planned to say, but it all disappeared from my mind. All I could do was lay my head on her breast and cry. I was a child again.

Kathy, the girls, and I would be there only three days. The first two days, I didn't have a chance to talk with Mom about spiritual things. There were too many other people around, and her strength ran out too quickly. On the third day, I asked Brett to take everyone back to the house and leave me alone with her. As we talked, she opened up and shared spiritual things. Roberta and I went to school with a man named Mitch Glaser, who now worked with Jews for Jesus. Mitch lived in San Francisco, and Roberta had let Mitch know our mother was there in the hospital.

Mom told me, "Your friend, Mitch, visited me a few months ago and I accepted Jesus as my Savior and Lord. I still have some questions though. I'm glad you are here to talk with me about them." Growing up as a Jew and then becoming a Jehovah's Witness when she married, she had questions about Bible doctrine, especially the Trinity.

"I just don't understand." She had said this before, but the statement no longer sounded defensive. Now it sounded like a plea for help.

"Mom, I don't understand it fully either." That wasn't the answer she expected. "There are many things in the Bible I don't understand, but I believe them because they're part of God's Word. I've learned not to concentrate on what I don't understand, when there is so much that is clear. God doesn't base salvation on our ability to understand, only on our faith in Him. In fact, the Bible says that the natural person cannot understand the things of the Spirit of God." I told her some of the stories of faith I had seen so recently among our Kayagar believers in Irian Jaya. "They didn't understand everything, but they trusted God."

"When did my boy grow up?" She patted my hand that held hers. "Remember the night you said you were going to become a preacher? You surely did."

"That's just what I did, Dave, I trusted God. I admitted to Him that I couldn't understand, but I couldn't put Him off because of that, either. Maybe I'll never understand it all, but understanding doesn't seem that important anymore."

Before leaving the house that morning, I had tucked Kristen's Good News Bible into my pocket. Mom saw it now and asked, "I've always wondered about the book of Hebrews. I'm Jewish so I suppose it was written for people like me. Would you read that to me now?"

I read to her through the rest of the afternoon. She fought sleep, but I knew it was time to leave. "Mom, the church in Hawthorne has an apartment waiting for us, and they expect us there tomorrow. Brett and Flora aren't set up to handle another family in their house. So, I have to go now, but I'm going to come back after I get my family set up in New Jersey. I'll stay with Brett and rent a car so I can come to the hospital and spend more time with you. I'll be back in a week or so, and we can read together again." I'm not good at good-byes, so I simply left with those words and that promise.

That was the last time I saw my mother on this earth. A week later Brett phoned. "Mom died quietly two days ago. She used all her willpower to stay alive and see you last week. She made me promise not to tell you she was gone until I could carry out her instructions. She didn't want to inconvenience anyone with a funeral so she asked me to have her body cremated immediately and scatter her ashes in the Pacific Ocean. I've done that."

How like her. After Brett hung up, I stayed on the dead line as if talking directly to God. "Thank You, Lord, for letting me know I will see Mom again in heaven. And thank You," I whispered into the handset, "for letting me see her one last time."

Roberta had written to me a few weeks before that, "It's always sad to lose someone you love, but it's sweet to lose that person to God." Those words were suitable companions to the familiar verses that ran through my mind. "Death is swallowed up in victory" I Corinthians 15:54. And "For whatsoever is born of God overcometh the world: and this is the victory that overcometh the world, even our faith" I John 5:4.

During the death of a parent, people often take time to reflect on their lives. I was no exception. One day, in my mind's eye, I looked around my own circle of blessing. I saw:

My mother.
My father.
Taffy and Roberta, my sisters who prayed me into Bible college.
My brothers, Brett and Tim
Bruce Allen, the pastor who invited me to the Billy Graham film where I met Jesus.
Billy Graham who, even through a tape, shared the gospel message so clearly.
Kathy and others who prayed for me to be saved.
Charlie Roberts and others who discipled me.
Kathy's parents and other family members.
Friends who influenced both of our lives.
Our teachers at Bible college.
People at RBMU.
People who prayed for us while we served in Irian Jaya.
People who encouraged us with letters.
People who supported us financially.
People who helped me learn valuable lessons.
And the list went on and on...
Most important of all, I saw Jesus sitting at the right hand of the Father. He had given the ultimate blessing!

Without those who joined in my circle of blessing, I couldn't have played my role in God's plan; and I couldn't have passed on God's blessing to others.

I have had opportunities through the years to share my story with many people around the world, and now with you, the readers of this book. I pray that it has blessed you, encouraged you, and motivated you to praise God and pray for your missionaries and the people they serve. This is the story of one unreached people group which is now "reached" with the gospel, but there are many more around the world.

I wish I could hear each reader's story of how God has blessed you and how He has used you to bless others. I'll look forward to meeting you in heaven where there are no limits such as time and space—where people from every tribe and tongue will gather in victory to worship and praise the Lamb.

CHAPTER THIRTEEN APPLICATION GUIDE

Matthew Chapter Five suddenly becomes clear when we consider God's blessings to us and to others through us.

"Blessed are the poor in spirit; for theirs is the kingdom of heaven" Matthew 5:3. Dave turned to God when he realized he was spiritually bankrupt. God blessed him with an inheritance in heaven.

"Blessed are they that mourn; for they shall be comforted" Matthew 5:4. When Dave mourned for his sin, Jesus forgave him and comforted him. When Dave mourned for the lost people in Irian Jaya, God worked through Dave to bless the Kayagar and he was comforted.

"Blessed are the meek; for they shall inherit the earth" Matthew 5:5. When Dave learned to submit and quit relying on his own pride, God allowed him more authority and leadership.

"Blessed are they who hunger and thirst after righteousness; for they shall be filled" Matthew 5:6. When Dave quit trying to satisfy his own desires, God gave him a gratifying relationship with Him and others.

"Blessed are the merciful; for they shall obtain mercy" Matthew 5:7. When Dave showed love and mercy to the Kayagar and Autohoim, God created a close relationship between them and Dave. The people in Irian Jaya showed Dave love and mercy.

"Blessed are the pure in heart; for they shall see God" Matthew 5:8. When Dave had his heart in tune with God and followed His ways, he saw God with his spiritual eyes and knew God is real and present. He knew God is powerful and loving.

"Blessed are the peacemakers; for they shall be called the sons of God" Matthew 5:9. When Dave stepped into the circle of warriors ready for battle and shared with them God's peace, they recognized Dave's relationship with his heavenly Father. Wayrem's conversion was a blessed result.

PONDER these Scriptures:

Psalm 98:1; Isaiah 25:8; I Corinthians 15:54-57.

PRAISE God for victory over sin and death.

Read I Chronicles 29:11 as praise to the Lord.

Praise God for His mighty power.

PEER into your heart.

Is anything keeping you from running a victorious spiritual race?

Are you willing to get rid of these weights (sins)?

PRAYER

Almighty God, I praise You for Your everlasting triumph. Thank You for a living Savior Who overcame sin and death for me. I pray for those who are still chained by sin and fear. Please open their spiritual eyes so they will see Your mighty power. Please help caring Christians share Your gospel and help the lost find victory over Satanic powers and over their own flesh. I ask this in the Name of Jesus Christ, Who rose victorious from the grave. Amen.

Afterword

"Tomorrow the new missionary candidates arrive for training. I think I have my schedule ready and everything in order."

Listening to me planning aloud, Kathy remarked, "When you were one of these candidates thirteen years ago, did you ever think you would lead the Candidate School?"

Hers was a rhetorical question, but I couldn't help replying, "The real question is, 'Did the people leading it then think I would ever be candidate secretary for RBMU International?'"

Change could well be the one constant in the world. After nine years in Irian Jaya, we were becoming effective as tribal church planters. Now I was learning new responsibilities in the U.S. office. Kathy didn't even have a position. It would be over ten years before she and I worked in the same ministry again. Organizational change also directly affected our lives at this time. Shortly after our arrival, RBMU entered a growth phase, where, for a time, we saw growth of ten percent per year, double the average for most other missions. That growth led to some organizational restructuring. Growing pains are a good problem, but a problem nonetheless.

At its beginning in the nineteenth century, the Regions Beyond Missionary Union had been an agency centered in England. By the time I joined the U.S. staff, the mission had divided into four separate sending councils. The offices in Australia, Canada, and the United States continued working together as RBMU International, and also continued moving towards a more formal international structure. The changes brought growth; the growth brought changes—another circle of blessing—and challenges.

I remember standing outside the Administration Building of Columbia International University about 11:00 P.M. one day in early November of 1993. I was on this campus in South Carolina to recruit more missionaries for our needs around the world.

On this autumn night I looked around self-consciously to be sure I was alone, then began praying aloud. "Lord, something is happening. I can feel that you're trying to tell me something, but I don't know what it is. You've been giving me experiences beyond my normal responsibilities. You've been showing me open doors without pointing specifically to any one of them. Father, I think you're leading me somewhere. I'm content to wait if that's Your will, but please tell me something soon." As I went to my room that night I couldn't imagine how quickly God would act on my submission.

Within three months we left RBMU International, without knowing exactly where the Lord wanted to use us next. We didn't lack options. One church asked me to accept a position as missions pastor. Another invited me to apply as senior pastor. The dean of a respected Bible college contacted me to join their missions department faculty. Kathy and I wrestled with these and other options, but did not feel comfortable enough to say yes to any of them.

When we heard the phone ring one afternoon in early January, we had no way of knowing it was a call from God. "Hello, my name is David Wood. I'm the personnel director with SEND International. One of our representatives just told me you might be available to fill a position in our office."

By the time the call ended I was walking on air. Dave had said he didn't have time to talk that afternoon, but wanted to make sure I knew of his interest. We set a time to talk again the next morning. The result of that call was an invitation to visit SEND's campus in suburban Detroit, Michigan.

Kathy and I prepared for this meeting by learning as much as we could about SEND International. We learned that as World War II ended, a group of young service personnel became burdened for the spiritual needs of Asia. Even before they were demobilized, these men and women teamed with veteran missionaries, military chaplains and local believers to begin Bible studies and evangelistic meetings in the Philippines and Japan. From their burden grew the church-planting ministry known initially as the *Far Eastern Gospel Crusade* (FEGC), now SEND International. While continuing to plant churches in the original fields of Japan, Taiwan, the Philippines, Hong Kong, and Alaska/Yukon, SEND International has followed God's leading in the last decade into ministry in Europe and the former Soviet Union.

Two weeks later I found myself sitting with all the SEND North American staff as part of the Annual Planning Retreat. I had no real part in the planning. As an observer, I could concentrate on the people around me. How would they interact with each other? What was on their hearts? Most importantly, could I work with them comfortably and effectively?

In one of the early planning sessions, an invited business consultant lectured about organizational *flow*. He encouraged the staff of SEND to think of the *input* to each department or function as well as the *output*. Even though I was not yet part of this group, I tried to apply what I was hearing. *If I accept this position,* I thought to myself, *I will be recruitment director. Input will be people who are considering missionary service, output will be new missionaries. That sounds simple enough.*

Then the lecturer turned to Frank Severn. "Frank, what is the output of your role as general director of this mission?"

With no hesitation, Frank responded with one word. "Vision."

My heart rang in harmony to his single word. Here was a man, a leader, who would help all of us see and understand God's direction for SEND and would inspire us to move in that direction. I relaxed and knew that I had found God's direction for the next years of my life.

I accepted the position at SEND and our family moved to southeast Michigan in 1994. Our daughters Gwen and Kristen had just graduated, Gwen from Liberty University and Kris from Abington High School. Gwen would live with Kathy and me another year before her wedding, while Kristen soon went off to her studies at Moody Bible Institute in Chicago. I fit easily and, I trust, effectively, into my new responsibilities. Within a year, Kathy was also offered a position in SEND's International Office. For the first time since leaving Irian Jaya in 1984, Kathy and I were working together in one ministry.

As I look back over our ministry in Irian Jaya and the years since, I can see how God moved through our lives. He used us, true, but also used the experiences you've just read about to help prepare me for the place I am now. And now, with the help of Arlene Knickerbocker, I've written a book. Writing, though, will never become my first priority. This is a tool to tell you what God is doing in our world. The calling God has given me since leaving the mission field is to mobilize and equip His people in North America to carry on the task of planting His Church around the world. I'm glad that you have read *Circles of Blessing: Redemption in the Rain Forest.* I will be even more glad to see how God uses these words to mobilize you for His task of world evangelization.

Dear reader, if you would like to use your prayers, your finances, your life to touch our world for Jesus Christ, here are some suggestions. You might want to begin gathering information on mission opportunities. I can immediately recommend two great mission agencies. You've already read a lot about RBMU International. RBMU has merged with Worldteam to form a new mission agency, World Team, which I highly recommend. Look for them at "*www.worldteam.org*" This afterward has introduced you to SEND International. You can contact SEND at "*www.send.org*" for basic information and counsel.

If you would like to contact me personally, I would be honored to be part of your circle of blessing. May God bless and use you.

David A. Tucker
SEND International
P. O. Box 513
Farmington, MI 48332.

DTucker@send.org